KOMPAKT-WISSEN ENGLISCH

Maria G

4X

Rainer Jacob

Grundwortschatz

STARK

ISBN 978-3-86668-005-0

D-85318 Freising · Postfach 1852 · Tel. (0 81 61) 1790

Inhalt

Autor: Rainer Jacob

Vorwort

Liebe Schülerin, lieber Schüler,

du hast sicher schon gemerkt, wie wichtig ein umfangreicher Wortschatz ist; egal, ob es darum geht, einen Text zu verstehen, Fragen zu beantworten oder selbst Texte zu verfassen. Mit diesem Band kannst du die 1000 wichtigsten Vokabeln und Idioms ganz leicht lernen oder wieder auffrischen. Somit bist du optimal auf den Unterricht und auf Klassenarbeiten vorbereitet.

Der übersichtliche Aufbau erleichtert dir die Arbeit:

- Die **Vokabeln** zu den wichtigsten im Unterricht behandelten Themen findest du **übersichtlich und thematisch geordnet** zusammengestellt. Als Wortfelder aufbereitet kannst du sie so leichter lernen. Zum Einprägen helfen dir auch die deutsche Bedeutung und der angegebene **Beispielsatz**: erst durch die Einbettung des Wortes in einen sinnvollen Zusammenhang siehst du, wie du das Wort verwenden kannst.
- Zum gezielten Nachschlagen und Wiederholen findest du am Ende des Buches eine **alphabetische Liste des kompletten Grundwortschatzes**, sowie der wichtigsten **unregelmäßigen Verben**. Somit kannst du eventuelle Lücken ganz schnell schließen.

Um gezielt einzelne Kapitel zu wiederholen, gehe Wort für Wort vor und bilde selbst englische Sätze, die du mit den angegebenen Beispielsätzen vergleichst. Wenn du deinen gesamten Wortschatz auffrischen willst, lies dir die Beispielsätze durch oder decke einzelne Spalten ab. Auch wenn du in der Schule bis jetzt noch nicht alle Wörter gelernt haben solltest, kannst du mit deinem neuen Buch arbeiten: wiederhole die, die du schon kennst und versuche dir auch ein paar neue Vokabeln einzuprägen. Ich bin mir sicher, dass du sie sehr bald brauchen kannst.

Jetzt wünsche ich dir viel Erfolg für deine Klassenarbeiten und vor allem viel Spaß beim Erweitern und Auffrischen deines Wortschatzes!

Rainer Jacob

Abkürzungsverzeichnis

AE	American English
BE	British English
am	vormittags
pm	nachmittags
jmdm.	jemandem
jmdn.	jemanden
Pl.	Plural

Family and Friends

vocabulary	dt. Bedeutung	English sentence
alone	*allein*	I don't like being alone at home.
aunt	*Tante*	My mother's or my father's sister is my aunt.
birth	*Geburt*	On December 24, people in Germany celebrate the birth of Jesus.
(to) give birth	*zur Welt bringen*	His mother gave birth to four children.
birthday	*Geburtstag*	My birthday is in December.
boy	*Junge*	Are you for classes with only boys?
boyfriend	*Freund*	Malcolm is Wendy's boyfriend.
brother	*Bruder*	Poppy has two brothers, Simon and Felix.
(to) break up	*zerbrechen, auseinandergehen*	The marriage between Diana and Charles broke up after 15 years.
bride	*Braut*	The bride looked lovely in her white dress.
bridegroom	*Bräutigam*	The bridegroom was very nervous.
child children [Pl.]	*Kind* *Kinder*	Children are our future.
couple	*Paar*	Marc and Lena are a nice couple.
cousin	*Cousin(e)*	My cousin Phil is the son of my aunt Jemma.
dad	*Papa*	If I want to know something I can always ask my dad.
date of birth	*Geburtsdatum*	My sister's date of birth is 3 January, 1998.
daughter	*Tochter*	The Millers have two daughters: Edwina and Lena.

vocabulary	dt. Bedeutung	English sentence
(to) divorce divorced	*sich scheiden lassen* *geschieden*	When Sue was twelve her parents divorced.
(to) get engaged	*verlobt*	When people get engaged they want to marry soon.
family	*Familie*	My mother's family was very poor.
family member	*Familienangehörige(r)*	At my grandmother's birthday all the family members come together.
father	*Vater*	My father works in the city.
favour	*Gefallen, Gefälligkeit*	Could you please do me a favour?
first name	*Vorname*	Three girls in my class have the same first name: Amy.
friend	*Freund(in)*	Nobody wants to be without friends.
friendly	*freundlich*	Friendly people smile a lot.
friendship	*Freundschaft*	My friendship to Tom began when we were seven.
gentleman	*Herr, Kavalier, Gentleman*	My grandfather is a real gentleman: he always lets ladies pass first.
girl	*Mädchen*	There's a new girl in my class.
girlfriend	*Freundin*	Chris has found a new girlfriend.
granddad	*Opa*	My granddad gave me an extra £ 10.
grandchild [ai]	*Enkelkind*	Our neighbour, Mr Myers, has twelve grandchildren.
granddaughter	*Enkelin*	The granddaughter of Mr Jones is only two years old.
grandfather	*Großvater*	I usually call my grandfather "granddad".
grandmother	*Großmutter*	My grandmother is my grandfather's wife.
grandparents	*Großeltern*	My mum's or my dad's parents are my grandparents.

vocabulary	dt. Bedeutung	English sentence
grandson	*Enkel*	Mr Keenan is very proud of his grandson.
honeymoon	*Flitterwochen*	Many people spend their honeymoon on the Hawaiian islands.
husband	*Ehemann*	Mr and Mrs Miller are husband and wife.
kid	*Kind, Jugendliche(r)*	Some toys are not only for kids.
lady	*Dame*	Yesterday I helped an old lady across the road.
(to) live together	*zusammen leben*	Today many couples live together even if they are not married.
(to) make friends	*Freundschaft schließen*	Brian is a very friendly boy and that's why he makes friends very quickly.
(to) be married	*verheiratet*	My sister has been married for two years now.
(to) marry	*heiraten*	Sue doesn't want to marry before she is 25.
member	*Mitglied*	I'm a member of our football club.
mother	*Mutter*	My mother comes from Scotland.
neighbour	*Nachbar(in)*	We help our neighbours and they help us, too.
nephew	*Neffe*	Harry is the son of my sister Jane. He is my nephew.
niece	*Nichte*	Hillary is the daughter of my brother Ed. She is my niece.
old	*alt*	How old are you?
older	*älter*	When I'm older I want to be a doctor.
parents	*Eltern*	My parents are quite strict and don't allow me to go out.
place of birth	*Geburtsort*	New York is Stuart's place of birth.

vocabulary	dt. Bedeutung	English sentence
(to) be related	*verwandt*	There are two pupils in my class who have the same family name; but they are not related.
relative	*Verwandte(r)*	My mother's relatives live in Kent.
(to) run in the family	*in der Familie liegen*	Jamie and his brothers are very musical. It runs in the family.
single	*ledig*	My brother Jimmy does not want to marry. He wants to stay single.
sister	*Schwester*	My sister likes music and ballet.
son	*Sohn*	The Learys have three sons and two daughters.
(to) start a family	*eine Familie gründen*	Leo and Zoe have got married and want to start a family soon.
twin	*Zwilling*	Louise and Jemma are twins; they look very much alike ("ähnlich").
uncle	*Onkel*	My uncle is a bus driver in Glasgow.
wedding	*Hochzeit*	The wedding of Princess Elizabeth and Prince Philip took place in Westminster Abbey in 1947.
wedding anniversary	*Hochzeitstag*	My parents' wedding anniversary is in march.
widow	*Witwe*	Mr Getty married a rich widow.
wife	*Ehefrau*	Mr Potter's wife Karin comes from Germany.
woman	*Frau*	I often help the little old woman who lives next door.
young	*jung*	Disneyland is an interesting place for young people.
youth	*Jugend; Jugendliche(r)*	At youth clubs young people can meet friends and try new activities.

At Home

vocabulary	dt. Bedeutung	English sentence
address	*Adresse*	Don't forget to give me your new address.
apartment	*Wohnung*	My brother James lives in an apartment in Westminster.
armchair	*Sessel*	Uncle Ben often sleeps in his arm-chair.
at the back	*hinten*	We have a little garden at the back of our house.
at the front	*vorn*	My dad parks his car at the front of our house.
balcony	*Balkon*	From our balcony we can see the whole town.
bath (to) have a bath	*Bad, (Bade)Wanne* *ein Bad nehmen*	When I feel cold, I have a hot bath.
bathroom	*Bad(ezimmer)*	My sister spends lots of hours in the bathroom.
bed	*Bett*	My bed is very comfortable.
bedroom	*Schlafzimmer*	Our house is small; that's why my brother Simon and I must share a bedroom.
bell (to) ring the bell	*Glocke, Klingel* *klingeln*	Our postman rings the bell when he has a parcel for us.
bench	*Bank (zum Sitzen)*	I was sitting on a bench by the river.
block of flats	*Wohnhaus, Mietshaus*	They are building a new block of flats next to our house.
board	*Brett*	Marc puts his Warhammer figures on a large board.
bookshelf	*Bücherregal*	There is a flower pot on my bookshelf.

vocabulary	dt. Bedeutung	English sentence
carpet	*Teppich*	My mother cleans our carpet with a special shampoo.
chair	*Stuhl*	Keep still – don't fall off your chair.
chest of drawers	*Kommode*	My father keeps his T-shirts in an old chest of drawers.
clock	*Uhr*	We have two clocks in our kitchen.
coffee table	*Couchtisch*	Tea and cake are served on a coffee table in the living room.
cooker	*Herd*	What do you prefer: the cooker or the microwave?
corner	*Ecke*	I have a TV set in the corner of my room.
corridor	*Flur*	We hang up our coats in the corridor.
cup	*Tasse*	Everyone in our family has his favourite cup.
cupboard	*Schrank*	Our kitchen cupboard is full of cups, saucers and plates.
curtain	*Vorhang*	Close the curtains. It's getting dark.
cutlery	*Besteck*	We keep cutlery in a big drawer ("Schublade").
desk	*Schreibtisch*	I do my homework at a desk in my room.
dining-room	*Esszimmer*	When we have lunch we sit in the dining-room around a big table.
dish	*Schale, Schüssel*	There are three apples in the glass dish on the coffee table.
dishes	*Geschirr*	I don't like washing the dishes by hand. I prefer the dishwasher.
dishwasher	*Geschirrspüler*	My sister usually loads the dish-washer.
door	*Tür*	Please shut the door.

vocabulary	dt. Bedeutung	English sentence
double bed	*Doppelbett*	My parents sleep in a double bed.
downstairs	*unten (im Haus), treppab, die Treppe hinunter*	On Sundays I always come downstairs in my pyjamas.
dustbin	*Mülleimer*	Our dustbin is always very full.
elevator	*Aufzug*	Do you use the elevator or the stairs?
entrance	*Eingang*	A large tree stands at the entrance to our house.
equipment	*Ausstattung*	Some sports equipment is expensive.
first floor	[BE] *erster Stock* [AE] *Erdgeschoss*	The British word "ground floor" means "first floor" in America.
flat	*Wohnung*	Marc and Lena move into their new flat in Kensington.
floor	*Fußboden*	The floor is covered with books and papers.
fork	*Gabel*	Don't eat with your fingers – use a fork.
fridge	*Kühlschrank*	We keep milk in the fridge.
front door	*Haustür*	The paperboy leaves newspapers at our front door.
garage	*Garage*	The Growneys have two garages for their cars.
garden	*Garten*	My grandfather likes working in the garden on Sundays.
(to) get up	*aufstehen*	I get up at half past six.
glass	*Glas*	Careful with that glass – it breaks easily.
ground floor	*Erdgeschoss*	Older people like to live in flats on the ground floor.
hall	*Flur, Diele*	My father painted our hall yellow.

vocabulary	dt. Bedeutung	English sentence
home	*Zuhause, Heim*	My home is my castle.
homeless	*heimatlos, obdachlos*	Homeless people often sleep in the streets or under bridges.
(to) be homesick	*Heimweh haben*	I am never homesick.
house	*Haus*	Our house is twelve years old.
household	*Haushalt*	My mum looks after our household.
housewife	*Hausfrau*	Being a housewife is not easy.
housework	*Hausarbeit*	I don't like housework.
key	*Schlüssel*	I must not lose my keys.
kitchen	*Küche*	Our kitchen is very large.
knife knives [Pl.]	*Messer*	Always be careful with sharp knives.
lamp	*(Steh)Lampe*	I like my new lamp – it is very bright.
(to) load the dishwasher	*die Spülmaschine einräumen*	Load the dishwasher and turn it on.
letterbox	*Briefkasten*	Our letterbox is always full of junk mail ("Reklamesendungen").
living room	*Wohnzimmer*	My grandmother buys fresh flowers for the living room.
lunch	*Mittagessen*	We have lunch at 1 o'clock.
mess	*Unordnung*	My mum says my room is a complete mess.
microwave	*Mikrowellenherd*	Heat it up in the microwave.
mobile phone	*Handy, Mobiltelefon*	All my friends have a mobile phone.
mug	*Becher*	Most English people drink their tea out of a mug.
neighbour	*Nachbar(in)*	We always help our neighbours.
neighbourhood	*Nachbarschaft*	We live in a friendly neighbourhood.
office	*Büro*	My father has his office in our house.

vocabulary	dt. Bedeutung	English sentence
pet	*Haustier*	Pets are not allowed here.
phone (to) be on the phone	*Telefon* *telefonieren*	My sister is always on the phone for hours.
piano	*Klavier*	My brother plays the piano.
plant	*Pflanze*	There is a beautiful plant on the balcony.
plate	*Teller*	Ralph can eat a plate of sandwiches.
rubbish (to) take the rubbish out	*Müll* *den Müll hinausbringen*	I always take the rubbish out.
saucer	*Untertasse*	You don't find "flying saucers" in a kitchen – they are up in the sky!
scissors	*Schere*	Please hand me the scissors.
shelf shelves [Pl.]	*Regal* *Regale*	My father put up a new shelf for my schoolbooks.
shopping (to) do the shopping	*Einkauf* *einkaufen gehen*	In America, there are huge shopping malls ("Einkaufszentren").
shower (to) have a shower	*Dusche* *sich duschen*	I have a cold shower every morning to be fit for the day.
space	*Raum, Platz*	There is not much space in my little bedroom.
spoon	*Löffel*	Spoon, fork and knife are called "cutlery".
staircase	*Treppenhaus*	The staircase in our house has 32 steps.
stairs	*Treppe*	My mum runs up and down the stairs all day.
storey	*Etage*	The Empire State Building has 102 stories.

vocabulary	dt. Bedeutung	English sentence
table (to) lay the table	*Tisch* *den Tisch decken*	Please help me lay the table.
telephone	*Telefon*	Almost everybody has a telephone in the house today.
television, TV (to) watch TV TV set	*Fernsehen* *fernsehen* *Fernsehgerät*	I am only allowed to watch TV from 6 to 7 pm.
tidy	*sauber*	Please keep your room tidy.
(to) tidy (up)	*aufräumen, säubern*	Before the winter starts we tidy up the garden.
toilet	*Toilette*	We have three toilets in our house.
tool	*Werkzeug*	My father keeps all his tools in a blue box.
toolbox	*Werkzeugkasten*	I often play with my father's toolbox.
umbrella	*Regenschirm*	When it rains I go out with an umbrella.
upstairs	*oben (im Haus)*	In our house there are three rooms upstairs.
wall	*Mauer, Wand*	I put up a new poster on my wall.
wallpaper	*Tapete*	Do you like the wallpaper in my room?
wardrobe	*Kleiderschrank*	There are too many coats in our wardrobe.
washbasin	*Waschbecken*	There are two washbasins in our bathroom.
(to) wash the dishes	*Geschirr spülen*	My aunt washes the dishes by hand.
window	*Fenster*	Please shut the window; it is too cold.
(to) wipe	*(ab)wischen*	Muriel wipes the dishes after lunch.

Body

vocabulary	dt. Bedeutung	English sentence
ankle	*Knöchel*	I've hurt my ankle playing football.
arm	*Arm*	Uncle Fred has a tattoo on his right arm.
back	*Rücken*	My dad carries my little brother on his back.
bald	*kahl*	My granddad lost his hair; his head is bald.
beard	*Bart*	Most pirates have long beards.
blind	*blind*	Blind people often have guide dogs.
blood	*Blut*	Do kings and queens have blue blood? Of course not!
body	*Körper*	Sportsmen have a fit body.
bone	*Knochen*	Drink milk to have strong bones.
(to) break	*brechen, sich etwas brechen*	Older people often break a leg or an arm.
(to) breathe	*atmen*	Breathe in the fresh air.
(to) brush	*bürsten, putzen*	Don't forget to brush your teeth.
cheek	*Wange*	Sandra's cheeks are rosy.
chest	*Brust, Brustkorb*	He crossed his arms over his chest.
chin	*Kinn*	What do we call the hair that grows on a man's chin? A beard, of course.
cold (to) catch a cold	*Erkältung* *sich erkälten*	Put something warm on or you will catch a cold!
cough (to) have a cough	*Husten*	Brian has a bad cough and has to stay at home.
(to) cut	*schneiden*	Be careful! Don't cut your finger with that big knife.

vocabulary	dt. Bedeutung	English sentence
dentist	*Zahnarzt, Zahnärztin*	Nobody likes going to the dentist's.
doctor	*Arzt, Ärztin*	A doctor comes to our school every six months.
ear	*Ohr*	Charles has big ears.
elbow	*Ellbogen*	Do not put your elbows on the table when you eat.
(to) examine	*untersuchen*	The doctor examines the baby.
eye	*Auge*	My granddad is blind in one eye.
face	*Gesicht*	I wash my face with cold water in the morning.
fair	*blond, hell*	Jane has fair hair.
fat	*dick*	Eating too much fast food can make you fat.
(to) feel sick	*übel sein*	Boat trips make me feel sick.
figure	*Figur*	Deborah has a slim figure.
finger	*Finger*	Don't play with fire. You will burn your fingers!
foot feet [Pl.]	*Fuß* *Füße*	I've been running around all day. My feet hurt.
hair	*Haar(e)*	Jennifer has long dark hair.
hand	*Hand*	My mum wears a ring on her left hand.
head	*Kopf*	"Please turn your head to the blackboard," the teacher said.
headache	*Kopfschmerzen*	When you play on your computer for hours you can get a headache.
health	*Gesundheit*	Most people care about their health.
healthy	*gesund*	How healthy are you?
heart	*Herz*	Mary has a weak heart.
height	*Körpergröße*	I am about 1.8 m (6 feet) in height.
hospital	*Krankenhaus*	Have you ever been to hospital?

vocabulary	dt. Bedeutung	English sentence
human	*menschlich*	The human body is a real miracle ("Wunder").
human being	*Mensch*	All human beings should have the same rights.
(to) hurt	*verletzen, sich verletzen*	Three people were hurt in the accident.
ill	*krank*	Phil is not at school: he is ill.
illness	*Krankheit*	Measles ("Masern") is an illness.
knee	*Knie*	Neil needs a knee operation.
large	*groß (und breit)*	A large diet coke, please.
lazy	*faul*	On Sundays I'm usually lazy.
leg	*Bein*	How long can you stand on one leg?
lip	*Lippe*	Women paint their lips red.
lungs	*Lunge*	Smoking is bad for your lungs.
medicine	*Medizin*	Some medicine tastes bitter.
mouth	*Mund*	"Please open your mouth wide," said the dentist.
muscle	*Muskel*	Sportsmen train their muscles.
neck	*Hals*	A giraffe has a very long neck.
nose	*Nase*	Many boxers have a broken nose.
nurse	*Krankenschwester*	Nora wants to be a nurse.
pain	*Schmerz*	I can feel a pain in my left leg.
(to) recover	*sich erholen, gesund werden*	I hope our teacher will recover from his operation soon.
rest (to) have a rest	*Ruhe(pause)* *sich ausruhen*	After doing hard work you must have a rest.
shoulder	*Schulter*	When I was young my dad sometimes carried me piggyback ("huckepack") on his shoulder.

vocabulary	dt. Bedeutung	English sentence
(to) weigh	*wiegen*	Many teenagers weigh far too much because they eat too much fast food.
sick (to) feel sick	*krank* *sich schlecht fühlen, übel sein*	Benny ate too many sweets. He now feels sick.
skin	*Haut*	Use a good cream to have soft skin.
skinny	*mager, dürr*	Children in poor countries are often very skinny.
slim	*schlank*	If you want to stay slim, you must not eat too much.
stomach	*Magen*	When I am nervous I can feel it in my stomach.
tall	*groß*	How tall are you?
thin	*dünn*	I think some models are too thin.
throat	*Kehle*	Your throat feels dry when you are thirsty.
thumb	*Daumen*	The baby often puts his thumb into his mouth.
toe	*Zehe*	The footballer broke the big toe on his right foot.
tongue	*Zunge*	“Please show me your tongue,” the doctor said.
tooth teeth [Pl.]	*Zahn* *Zähne*	Don’t eat too many sweets. They are bad for your teeth.
toothbrush	*Zahnbürste*	I use my toothbrush twice a day.
toothache	*Zahnschmerzen*	Harry has a terrible toothache.
treat	*behandeln*	A doctor will treat Linda’s broken leg.

Everyday Life

vocabulary	dt. Bedeutung	English sentence
afternoon	*Nachmittag*	In the afternoon we play hockey.
at school	*in der Schule*	English children are at school from 9 o'clock to 4 o'clock.
at work	*bei der Arbeit*	My father is at work from 9 to 5.
bag	*Tasche*	Pack your bag, we are leaving.
(to) be home	*zu Hause sein*	I'm normally home by half past four.
boot	*Stiefel*	In winter I wear warm boots.
boss	*Chef(in)*	My father's boss is a strict man.
break (to) have a break	*Ruhepause* *sich ausruhen*	After lunch I usually have a break.
breakfast	*Frühstück*	A cannot eat anything at breakfast.
building	*Gebäude, Bau*	In New York there are big buildings.
busy	*beschäftigt*	My father is always very busy.
butter	*Butter*	Do you like butter on your bread?
(to) buy	*kaufen*	My mum buys fresh fruit at the market.
cake	*Kuchen*	I like all sorts of cake.
care	*Betreuung, Aufmerksamkeit*	Babies need a lot of care.
(to) care about	*sich kümmern um*	Mrs Keenan cares about poor people in Africa.
careful	*vorsichtig*	Mr James is careful with money.
(to) carry	*tragen*	On Saturday I carry my mum's heavy shopping bags.
(to) catch (a bus, a train)	*erreichen*	Mr Williams catches the bus at 6:30.
cereals	*Frühstückszerealien (Cornflakes, Müsli)*	Do you like cereals or toast for breakfast?

vocabulary	dt. Bedeutung	English sentence
clean	*sauber*	I like a clean, not a dirty bedroom.
(to) clear up	*aufräumen*	Mrs Maddox always tells Freddy to clear up his room.
comb	*Kamm*	My sister Jenny has four different combs.
comfortable	*bequem*	My bed is very comfortable.
(to) congratulate	*gratulieren, beglückwünschen*	On my birthday, all my friends and family congratulate me.
congratulation	*Glückwunsch*	Congratulations on your good school report!
(to) cook	*kochen*	Boys should also learn to cook.
cook	*Koch, Köchin*	My mother is the best cook in the world.
(to) cut	*schneiden*	We have a bread cutter to cut the bread.
day	*Tag*	What day of the week is it?
daytime	*Tageszeit, am Tag*	I'm very busy in the daytime.
dear	*liebe(r)*	Dear Gary, how are you?
dish	*Schüssel, Schale, Platte; Gericht*	Soup is served in a big dish. My parents' favourite Indian dish is too hot ("scharf") for me.
dishes	*Geschirr*	We don't have to wash the dishes; we have a dishwasher.
(to) do one's homework	*Hausaufgaben machen*	English kids can do their homework at school in the afternoon.
(to) do the shopping	*Einkäufe machen*	My mum does the shopping in the morning when I am at school.
doctor	*Arzt*	My arm hurts; I must see a doctor.
dog	*Hund*	Our dog Brandy is a real watchdog: he barks when somebody is coming.
domestic	*häuslich, Haus-*	My mother would like a domestic help.

vocabulary	dt. Bedeutung	English sentence
dress	*Kleid*	My sister's favourite dress is pink.
(to) dress (to) get dressed	*sich anziehen*	My sister takes hours to get dressed.
drink (to) have a drink	*Getränk* *etwas trinken*	I'm thirsty ("durstig") – I must have a drink.
(to) drive	*fahren*	Drive slowly, the roads are icy.
(to) dry	*trocknen*	In summer we dry the washing in the fresh air.
dust	*Staub*	My old CDs are covered with dust.
evening in the evening	*Abend* *abends*	In the evening, after homework, I can finally relax.
favourite	*Lieblings-*	My favourite TV show is shown at 6:30 p.m.
(to) feel	*fühlen*	My father often feels tired when he gets home from work.
figure	*Figur*	Eat less to keep a slim ("schlank") figure.
(to) finish	*zu Ende sein, beenden*	School finishes at 4 in the afternoon.
fire	*Feuer*	Please stay away from the fire.
food	*Essen, Nahrung*	Eat healthy food and stay fit.
fruit	*Obst*	We buy fresh fruit every week.
garden	*Garten*	My granddad likes working in the garden.
(to) get dressed	*sich anziehen*	In the morning I get dressed very quickly.
(to) get ready	*sich fertig machen*	Come on, get ready; it's time to go!
(to) get up	*aufstehen*	At 6:30 my mum comes into my room and tells me to get up.
(to) go by bus	*mit dem Bus fahren*	Most of my classmates go to school by bus.
(to) go to bed	*zu Bett gehen*	I usually go to bed at half past nine.

vocabulary	dt. Bedeutung	English sentence
(to) greet	*grüßen*	When you greet an English friend you say "Hello, how are you?".
half past (eight)	*halb (neun)*	I get off the bus at half past eight.
healthy	*gesund*	Eat good food and stay healthy.
(to) help	*helfen*	I help the old lady in our house with her shopping.
Help yourself.	*Bediene Dich! Greif zu!*	Help yourself to another piece of cake.
cannot help doing sth.	*nicht anders können; einfach müssen*	I could not help laughing when he came in with these pink trousers.
honey	*Honig*	It's real Canadian honey.
hospital	*Krankenhaus*	My aunt works in a hospital; she is a nurse.
house	*Haus*	In 1992 my parents bought a house in Arizona.
housewife	*Hausfrau*	My mother is a housewife.
hungry	*hungrig*	My friend Bernie is always hungry.
income	*Einkommen*	Brian's father does not earn much money. His income is low.
jam	*Marmelade*	Jam is usually sweet and red; marmalade is made from oranges.
(to) be late	*zu spät kommen*	I try not to be late for school.
(to) leave for school	*zur Schule gehen*	I usually leave for school at 7 in the morning.
(to) leave (to) leave school	*verlassen* *die Schule verlassen*	When Stella leaves school she wants to work in a hotel.
(to) be left	*übrig sein*	Is there any cake left?
(to) look after	*sich kümmern um*	Mrs Mills looks after her two little children.
lunch	*Mittagessen*	More and more pupils are having lunch at the school canteen.

vocabulary	dt. Bedeutung	English sentence
(to) make the beds	*die Betten machen*	My mother makes the beds.
meal	*Mahlzeit, Essen, Gericht*	We have our evening meal at half past six. On Sundays we normally go out for a meal.
(to) go out for a meal	*essen gehen*	
(to) meet	*treffen*	At the weekend I meet my friends.
midday	*Mittag*	My grandparents have something warm to eat at midday.
(to) miss	*vermissen*	I miss my best friend: she has moved to Cardiff.
(to) miss	*verpassen*	Hurry up, or we will miss the bus!
morning	*Morgen*	I'm always tired in the morning.
(to) move	*sich bewegen*	Don't just stand there. Move!
(to) move	*umziehen*	The Growneys moved to Somerset.
night	*Nacht*	In winter the nights are longer.
nighttime	*Nacht*	It was already nighttime when we came back from our walk.
tonight	*heute Abend*	There is a good film on TV tonight.
nurse	*Krankenschwester*	Juliet wants to be a nurse.
postman	*Briefträger, Postbote*	Our postman is called Pat O'Neil.
(to) prepare	*vorbereiten*	I help my mother to prepare lunch.
(to) read	*lesen*	My brother Marc always reads in bed.
(to) repair	*reparieren*	My dad repairs my bike for me.
(to) ride a bike	*mit dem Fahrrad fahren*	Leo rides a bike to school.
(to) run	*rennen*	Jack is good at running.
shopping	*Einkaufen*	I don't like shopping very much.
shower	*Dusche*	A quick cold shower in the morning is a good start into the day.
(to) have a shower	*sich duschen*	I usually have a shower after sport.

vocabulary	dt. Bedeutung	English sentence
(to) start	*beginnen*	School usually starts around 9 o'clock in England.
(to) start on sth.	*mit etwas anfangen*	Have you started on your homework yet?
sun	*Sonne*	Our cat lies in the sun.
sunny	*sonnig*	My room is very sunny and bright.
supper	*Abendessen*	We don't eat much for supper.
(to) sweat	*schwitzen*	When it is hot we sweat.
(to) take s.o. to school	*jdn. in die Schule bringen*	Mrs Myers takes her two daughters to school every day.
(to) take to the post	*zur Post bringen*	Please take this letter to the post for me.
(to) take time	*Zeit kosten, dauern*	Doing all my homework takes time.
(to) tidy	*sauber machen*	I always tidy my room myself.
time	*Zeit*	It's time to go home.
What time is it?	*Wie spät ist es?*	Can you tell me what time it is?
(to) be on time	*pünktlich sein*	My school bus is nearly always on time.
(to) have a good time	*sich amüsieren*	We had a really good time on our holiday in Ireland.
tools	*Werkzeug*	My granddad has a lot of gardening tools.
(to) walk	*laufen, gehen, spazieren gehen*	Muriel lives next to our school; that's why she can walk to school.
(to) watch TV	*fernsehen*	I mustn't watch too much TV.
(to) work	*arbeiten*	Mr Newey works in a bank in the city.

School and School Life

vocabulary	dt. Bedeutung	English sentence
(to) achieve	*erreichen*	Harry studied a lot and achieved good marks in English.
(to) add up	*zusammenzählen*	Can you add up these numbers?
A-levels	*(etwa) Abitur*	After my A-levels I am going to study at a famous university.
angry	*zornig, wütend*	Don't be angry with me.
annoyed	*verärgert*	When we talk too much our teacher gets annoyed.
(to) answer	*beantworten, Antwort*	Try to answer all questions in the test paper.
(to) argue	*sich streiten*	Some of my friends argue a lot.
at school	*in der Schule*	I like being at school.
average	*Durchschnitt, durchschnittlich*	I am proud that my marks are better than average.
back	*zurück*	After the holidays we go back to school.
(to) be in charge of	*verantwortlich sein für, Verantwortung tragen*	A headmaster is in charge of a school.
biology	*Biologie*	Our biology teacher shows us lots of plants and animals.
board/ blackboard	*Tafel*	Write the new word on the board. Use blue chalk.
boarding school	*Internat*	English families often send their children to boarding schools.
book	*Buch*	Open your books at page 5.
(to) borrow	*ausleihen*	Can I borrow your pencil, please?
bully	*Rüpel, gemeine(r) Mitschüler(in)*	Barry is a great bully. We all hate him.

vocabulary	dt. Bedeutung	English sentence
bullying	*Tyrannisieren, Ärgern, Einschüchtern von Mitschülern*	Bullying makes life at school very difficult for some boys and girls.
career	*berufliche Laufbahn, Karriere*	Juliet dreams of a career as a model.
chalk	*Kreide*	Chalk comes in different colours.
chemistry	*Chemie*	Our chemistry teacher often makes interesting experiments.
choice	*Auswahl*	Learning Spanish was a good choice.
(to) choose	*wählen*	I would like to choose some of my school subjects.
class	*(Schul)Klasse*	There are 25 pupils in my class.
classmate	*Klassenkamerad(in)*	I like all my classmates.
classroom	*Klassenzimmer*	Our classroom has five windows.
(to) copy	*abschreiben, kopieren*	You must not copy from your neighbour.
(to) correct **correction**	*korrigieren* *Verbesserung*	Daniel corrects the mistakes of his English dictation.
course **(to) do a course**	*Kurs* *einen Kurs besuchen*	Gregory is doing an evening course to learn German.
day out	*(Tages)Ausflug*	Last Tuesday we had a day out at the zoo.
desk	*Schreibtisch*	My writing desk is always full of books and papers.
dictionary	*Wörterbuch*	Look up the new word in a dictionary.
disappointed	*enttäuscht*	Catherine is disappointed about her marks in maths.
(to) do homework	*Hausaufgaben machen*	Simon does his homework before he watches TV.
(to) do well	*gut abschneiden*	Students work hard to do well in their tests.

vocabulary	dt. Bedeutung	English sentence
drama group	*Theatergruppe*	I am a member of our drama group at school.
(to) draw	*zeichnen*	Children love drawing pictures.
drawing	*Zeichnung*	Pablo Picasso is famous for his drawings.
(to) drop out of school	*die Schule abbrechen, vorzeitig verlassen*	Unfortunately, too many black kids drop out of school in America.
education	*Ausbildung, Bildung*	Parents want a good education for their children.
(to) enter	*eintreten*	In 1995 Prince William entered Eton College.
eraser	*Radiergummi*	The British say "rubber", the Americans "eraser".
exam (ination)	*Prüfung*	I'll take my last exam in July and then I can enjoy my holidays.
example	*Beispiel*	The short form of "for example" is "i. e".
(to) set an example	*ein Beispiel geben*	Mike has always set his younger brother a good example.
exchange programme	*Austauschprogramm*	I am going to take part in an exchange programme for young people.
excursion	*Ausflug, Exkursion*	The class went on an excursion to Windsor Castle.
exercise book	*Heft*	Open your exercise books, please.
experience	*Erfahrung*	Our trip to Ireland was a nice experience.
extra classes	*Nachhilfe*	Lesley has extra classes in maths.
(to) fail	*nicht bestehen, durchfallen*	I have worked hard; I'm sure I won't fail my exam in July.
(to) fall asleep	*einschlafen*	Wake up, Henry. Don't fall asleep.

vocabulary	dt. Bedeutung	English sentence
favourite	*Lieblings-*	What is your favourite subject at school?
(to) finish school	*die Schule beenden*	When I finish school I want to work and earn some money.
foreign language	*Fremdsprache*	Foreign languages are becoming more and more important today.
form teacher	*Klassenlehrer(in)*	Mr Greeves is our new form teacher.
geography	*Erdkunde, Geografie*	In geography we learnt that Australia once was a colony for prisoners.
(to) be good at	*gut sein in*	Celine is good at French.
grade [AE]	*(Schul)Klasse, Jahrgangsstufe*	The Americans say "grade" for "class" or "form".
(to) hate	*hassen*	I like school, but my older sister hates it.
headmaster	*Schulleiter(in)*	Mr Barnes is our new headmaster.
history	*Geschichte*	In history we learned about the Battle of Hastings.
holiday	*Ferien, Urlaub*	I am looking forward to the holidays.
homework	*Hausaufgaben*	Our maths teacher gives us a lot of homework.
homework diary	*Hausaufgabenheft*	I keep a homework diary so that I won't forget what I have to do.
(to) improve	*sich verbessern, besser machen/werden*	My Spanish is improving, because I spent my holidays in Madrid.
(to) interrupt	*unterbrechen*	Noisy children often interrupt the lessons.
language course	*Sprachkurs*	Au pair girls often go to language courses.
late	*spät*	In England schools starts late.
(to) be late	*zu spät kommen*	Kevin is sometimes late for school.

vocabulary	dt. Bedeutung	English sentence
(to) leave	*verlassen*	Most English pupils leave school when they are 16.
lesson	*Unterrichtsstunde, Lektion*	Every Tuesday we have two French lessons.
library	*Bücherei*	The library of Trinity College, Dublin, houses the famous Book of Kells.
(to) listen	*zuhören*	Listen carefully to what I say.
mark	*Schulnote*	Good marks are important to get a good job.
maths	*Mathe (Kurzform)*	Hannah is not good at maths.
mistake	*Fehler*	In our last English dictation I had 12 mistakes.
noisy	*laut*	Some classes are noisy.
note	*Notiz*	Leave a note on the kitchen table when you leave the house.
(to) take notes	*Notizen machen, mitschreiben*	While the history teacher tells about the First World War we must take notes.
oral	*mündlich*	In oral exams I am more nervous than in written exams.
page	*Seite*	Our new English book has 234 pages.
(to) pass	*(eine Prüfung) bestehen*	Things are going well. I've just passed my exams.
physical education (PE)	*(Schul)Sport, Sportunterricht*	We have PE on Tuesdays and Fridays.
pen fountain pen	*Feder, Füller*	Can you give me your pen, please? I cannot find mine.
pencil	*Bleistift*	Mr Norman always has a pencil behind his right ear.
pencil case	*Federmäppchen*	I have a new pencil case. It is red and blue.

vocabulary	dt. Bedeutung	English sentence
physics	*Physik*	Most pupils find physics difficult.
(to) prepare	*sich vorbereiten*	Students study and prepare for exams.
project	*Projekt, Vorhaben*	We'll start a new project about TV and comics next week.
pupil	*Schüler(in)*	There are 2,500 pupils at my school.
question	*Frage*	Try to answer the questions on the text.
quiet	*ruhig*	Our teacher often asks us to be quiet.
research **(to) do research**	*Forschung* *nachforschen, erforschen, untersuchen*	We sometimes do research on the internet.
rubber	*Radiergummi*	I've just made a mistake. Can I borrow your rubber, please?
ruler	*Lineal*	Use a ruler to draw a straight ("gerade") line.
school	*Schule*	In England school starts at 9 o'clock.
school fees	*Schulgeld, Schulgebühren*	At private schools pupils have to pay school fees.
school holiday(s)	*Schulferien*	In my school holidays I visit my aunt in Glasgow.
school meal	*(Mittag)Essen in der Schule*	Sally's favourite school meal is fish and chips.
school report	*Zeugnis*	My sister always gets a good school report.
school trip	*Schulfahrt, Klassenreise*	Many parents say that school trips are expensive.
school uniform	*Schuluniform*	At British schools children wear school uniforms.
sentence	*Satz*	Make five sentences with the verb "to take".

vocabulary	dt. Bedeutung	English sentence
skill	*Fähigkeit, Fertigkeit*	At school we learn the skills which will be useful later on.
(to) speak up	*lauter sprechen*	Can you please speak up so that the others can hear you?
speech	*Rede*	Martin L. King's speech "I have a dream" is quite a famous one.
(to) spell	*richtig schreiben*	How do you spell this word, please?
spelling	*Rechtschreibung*	Harold makes too many spelling mistakes in his dictations.
staff-room	*Lehrerzimmer*	Our teachers have a coffee machine in the staff-room.
strict	*streng*	Mr Greaves is a very strict teacher.
student	*Student(in), Schüler(in)*	Ian is a student at Oxford University.
(to) study	*lernen, studieren*	Jenny wants to have good marks; she studies very hard.
subject	*Schulfach*	History is my favourite subject.
(to) take an exam	*eine Prüfung machen*	British school children take their first exam when they are 7.
talent	*Begabung*	Daniel has creative talent. He writes music.
(to) test	*prüfen, testen; Klassenarbeit, Prüfung*	Test your English vocabulary!
textbook	*Lehrbuch*	Our new English textbook has a lot of pictures and cartoons.
timetable	*Stundenplan*	Next week we will get a new time-table.
uniform	*Uniform*	English schoolchildren wear uni-forms.
vocabulary	*Wortschatz, Vokabular*	We must learn the new vocabulary of unit 3.
worksheet	*Arbeitsblatt*	Try to do all the exercises on the worksheet.

Free Time and Hobbies

vocabulary	dt. Bedeutung	English sentence
active	*aktiv*	Most people want to be active in their free time.
activity	*(Freizeit)Beschäftigung im Freien; Tätigkeit*	Sports are an important school activity.
amazing	*erstaunlich*	The London Planetarium is an amazing place.
boring	*langweilig*	Some people find collecting stamps boring.
box office	*Kasse*	The box office opens at 6 o'clock.
canoeing	*Kanu fahren*	In the summer Julianne goes canoeing with her brother and father.
(to) collect	*sammeln*	Do you collect music CDs or DVDs?
(to) collect stamps	*Briefmarken sammeln*	Collecting stamps is an interesting hobby.
computer games	*Computerspiele*	Neil likes playing computer games.
cooking	*Kochen*	Cooking is my father's hobby.
(to) do aerobics	*Aerobic machen*	My neighbour does aerobics three times a week.
(to) do sport	*Sport treiben*	You should do more sport to keep fit.
entertaining	*unterhaltsam*	Many people find quiz shows on TV entertaining.
entertainment	*Unterhaltung*	Making films is an important entertainment industry.
equipment	*Ausrüstung*	I must buy new tennis equipment.
exciting	*spannend, aufregend*	Standing at the rim ("Rand") of the Grand Canyon is exciting.

vocabulary	dt. Bedeutung	English sentence
exercise	*(körperliche) Bewegung, Training, Gymnastik*	Jean does a lot of exercise every week.
(to) exercise	*trainieren, üben*	If you want to become better, you must exercise every day.
experience	*Erfahrung*	Our trip to Scotland was a beautiful experience.
favourite	*Lieblings-*	Reading books is Susan's favourite hobby.
(to) be fun	*Spaß machen*	A visit to the zoo is great fun.
game	*Spiel*	I like playing games with my friends.
gardening	*Gartenarbeit*	My mother likes gardening because of the fresh air.
(to) get away	*entfliehen, entkommen*	At weekends we often try to get away from the city.
(to) go (window) shopping	*Schaufensterbummel machen*	Especially around Christmas it's nice to go window shopping.
(to) go for a walk	*einen Spaziergang machen*	My grandfather goes for a walk in the afternoon.
health	*Gesundheit*	My grandmother worries about her health.
healthy	*gesund*	Keep your body fit and healthy!
helmet	*Helm*	Wear a helmet to protect your head.
indoors	*Hallen-*	On cold days we stay indoors.
inline-skating	*Inlineskate fahren*	Wear a helmet when you go inline-skating.
(to) be interested in	*Interesse haben an*	Most girls are interested in ballet and dancing.
invitation	*Einladung*	I sent an invitation to my classmates.
invite	*einladen*	I want to invite all my friends to my birthday party.
jogging	*Jogging*	When I go jogging I am always out of breath.

vocabulary	dt. Bedeutung	English sentence
(to) join	*beitreten, mitmachen*	I joined our school band.
(to) keep fit	*fit, gesund bleiben*	Meryl goes to a fitness centre three times a week to keep fit.
(to) keep s.o. waiting	*jdn. warten lassen*	When I have a meeting I am always on time. I don't want to keep people waiting.
leisure (time)	*Freizeit*	What interests do you have in your leisure time?
(to) listen to CDs	*CDs hören*	Ken's hobby is listening to CDs.
(to) look forward to	*sich freuen auf*	James and his sister Laura look forward to their trip to the sea.
(to) meet friends	*Freunde treffen*	I meet my friends in our youth club every Saturday.
member	*Mitglied*	Helena is a member of our youth club.
mobile phone	*Handy*	Even young kids have mobile phones today.
mountain biking	*Mountainbike fahren*	We go mountain biking in Scotland.
outdoors	*draußen, im Freien*	When it's warm we play outdoors.
(to) paint	*malen*	Painting pictures is not as easy as it seems.
pastime	*Zeitvertreib*	Chess is my favourite pastime.
pen friend	*Brieffreund(in)*	My French pen friend is called Michelle DuBois.
(to) phone friends	*Freunde anrufen*	Phoning your friends can be very expensive.
(to) play a musical instrument	*ein Musikinstrument spielen*	Playing a musical instrument can be very relaxing.
(to) play in a band	*in einer Band spielen*	My brother Christopher plays in our school band.

vocabulary	dt. Bedeutung	English sentence
(to) play on the computer	*am Computer spielen*	My mother says I play on my computer too often.
(to) play the guitar	*Gitarre spielen*	My friend Marc plays the guitar in a famous band.
(to) play the piano	*Klavier spielen*	Elton John does not only sing, he also plays the piano beautifully.
popular	*beliebt*	Walking is a popular free time activity.
(to) practise	*üben*	If you want to win, you have to practise hard.
(to) practise (a sport, hobby)	*ausüben*	Most teenagers like to practise a sport or hobby.
(to) relax	*sich entspannen*	Relax, take it easy.
(to) ride a bike	*Fahrrad fahren*	Riding a bike is much better for you than driving a car.
ule	*Regel, Vorschrift*	You must always keep to the rules of a game.
ight	*Sehenswürdigkeit*	Edinburgh Castle is a beautiful sight.
to) go sightseeing	*besichtigen*	Millions of tourists go sightseeing in London.
to) skateboard	*Skateboard fahren*	Skateboarding is a favorite activity of most boys.
leeping bag	*Schlafsack*	When you go camping, think of a warm sleeping bag.
tay	*Aufenthalt*	During our stay in London we went to Buckingham Palace.
to) stay at a hotel	*in einem Hotel wohnen*	Camping is more fun than staying at a hotel.
to) surf the Internet	*im Internet surfen*	Surfing the internet is not expensive any more today.
to) take a break	*eine Pause machen*	On our bike tour we take a break by the river.

vocabulary	dt. Bedeutung	English sentence
(to) take off	*starten*	Our plane takes off at 6 in the morning.
(to) take part in	*teilnehmen an*	All my friends will take part in our trip to Cornwall.
(to) take photos	*Fotos machen*	Sue takes photos for the school newspaper.
(to) take place	*stattfinden*	The Olympic Games take place every four years.
time	*Zeit*	I almost forgot what time it was.
(to) have a great time	*Spaß haben*	We had such a great time at the zoo.
tourism	*Tourismus*	Tourism brings money to poor countries.
tourist	*Tourist(in)*	Millions of tourists fly to far-away countries every year.
tourist attraction	*Touristenattraktion*	Disneyland is a tourist attraction.
(to) travel	*reisen*	In the summer we often travel to the Scottish Highlands.
viewer	*Zuschauer(in)*	All TV viewers like good films.
(to) visit	*besuchen*	On our trip to London we visited the Tower.
(to) watch birds	*Vögel beobachten*	My cousin watches birds and knows all their names.
(to) watch TV	*fernsehen*	My granddad's hobby is watching TV.
(to) work out	*trainieren*	My mother works out at the fitness centre.
youth club	*Jugendclub*	Kevin and his friends meet at the local youth club.
youth hostel	*Jugendherberge*	Our class stayed at a youth hostel in Devon.

Sport

vocabulary	dt. Bedeutung	English sentence
activity	*(Freizeit)Beschäftigung im Freien; Tätigkeit*	Sports are an important school activity.
athlete	*Athlet(in)*	Good athletes earn a lot of money.
athletics	*Leichtathletik*	British children can practise athletics at school.
(to) attract	*anziehen*	A Champions' League match always attracts lots of spectators.
attraction	*Attraktion, Sehenswürdigkeit*	The Scottish Highland Games are a major tourist attraction.
ball game	*Ballspiel*	Most kids like ball games.
bat	*Schläger*	A bat is a piece of wood that you use to hit the ball in some games, for example baseball.
(to) be fun	*Spaß machen*	Playing football with my friends is great fun.
(to) be on a team	*in einer Mannschaft sein*	Many girls would give everything to be on a cheerleading team.
(to) breathe	*atmen*	My mum likes going for a walk and breathe in the fresh air.
breath	*Atem*	After running I am usually out of breath.
boxing	*Boxen*	Boxing was Muhammad Ali's job.
canoeing	*Kanu fahren*	In the summer Julianne goes canoeing with her brother and father.
(to) celebrate	*feiern*	Our team celebrated the victory.
champion	*Sieger(in), Meister*	Michael Schumacher was a great champion.

vocabulary	dt. Bedeutung	English sentence
changing room	*Umkleidekabine*	After a football match our changing room is always a complete mess.
(to) cheer	*anfeuern*	The fans cheer and encourage their team.
(to) climb	*klettern, besteigen*	On May 29, 1953, Sir Edmund Hillary and Tenzing Norgay climbed Mount Everest for the first time.
coach	*Trainer(in)*	Jack Straw is my tennis coach.
(to) compete	*wetteifern, konkurrieren*	In hockey we compete with two other schools in the neighbourhood.
competition	*Wettkampf*	Heather takes part in the swimming competition.
competitor	*Konkurrent(in), Wettbewerber(in)*	Henry tries to be better than his competitor.
crowd	*Menschenmenge, Zuschauermenge*	There are always big crowds at international football matches.
cup final	*Pokalendspiel*	Manchester United won the cup final.
cycling	*Rad fahren*	My friend Jeremy goes cycling in the French alps.
(to) dive	*tauchen*	Do you know how to dive?
(to) do aerobics	*Aerobic machen*	My neighbour does aerobics three times a week.
(to) do sport	*Sport treiben*	Do more sport to keep fit.
draw	*Unentschieden*	The football match ended in a draw.
entrance	*Eintritt*	Entrance is free for children under 14.
equipment	*Ausrüstung*	Very good sportsmen get their equipment for free from sponsors.
event	*Ereignis*	The Tour de France is a famous cycling event.
exciting	*aufregend, spannend*	I find football matches exciting.

vocabulary	dt. Bedeutung	English sentence
famous	*berühmt*	Michael Jordan is a famous basketball player.
favourite	*Lieblings-*	Basketball is a favorite sport for boys.
(to) fight	*kämpfen* *Kampf*	Football fans sometimes fight after a match.
final	*Endspiel*	It is very hard to get into the final.
football	*Fußball*	All over the world people play football.
game	*Spiel*	Rugby is a rough game.
(to) have games	*Sport haben*	When do we have games?
ground	*Stadion*	FC Chelsea's home ground is called "Stamford Bridge".
gymnastics	*Turnen*	I sometimes watch gymnastics on TV.
hero heroes [Pl.]	*Held*	In 1967 Francis Chichester was the first man to sail alone around the world. He was a real hero.
heroine	*Heldin*	Lara Croft is a famous video game heroine.
hooligan	*Rowdy*	Young football hooligans get into trouble with the police.
(to) hit the ball	*den Ball schlagen, treffen*	Tennis players hit the ball hard.
indoor	*Innen-, Hallen-*	Squash is an indoor sport.
inline-skating	*Inlineskate fahren*	Jill and Daniel go inline-skating.
(to) join	*beitreten, mitmachen*	I joined our local swimming club.
(to) keep fit	*fit, gesund bleiben*	Meryl goes to a fitness centre three times a week to keep fit.
(to) kick (a ball)	*einen Ball spielen*	David Beckham knows how to kick a ball.
(to) kick s.o. off a team	*jdn. aus dem Team werfen*	John was never on time for the training. That's why he was kicked off the team.

vocabulary	dt. Bedeutung	English sentence
live	*direkt (TV- oder Radiosendung)*	Arsenal against Chelsea is shown live on TV.
manager	*Trainer(in)*	Mr Wilkinson is the manager of our football club.
match	*Spiel*	George is watching a football match.
member	*Mitglied*	Ralph is a member of Manchester United Football Club.
mountain biking	*Mountainbike fahren*	We go mountain biking in Scotland.
net	*Netz*	In tennis you have to play the ball over the net.
Olympic Games	*Olympische Spiele*	The Olympic Games began in Greece.
outdoors	*draußen, im Freien*	When it's warm we play outdoors.
(to) take part in	*teilnehmen*	All good sportsmen want to take part in the Olympic Games.
physical education (PE)	*Schulsport (in der Halle), Sportunterricht*	We have PE twice a week: on Mondays and Thursdays.
(to) play	*spielen*	I play volleyball every Friday afternoon.
playing field	*Spielfeld*	There are two playing fields behind our school building.
popular	*beliebt*	Football is very popular in England.
(to) practise (a sport, hobby)	*ausüben*	Most teenagers like to practise a sport or hobby.
professional	*Profi-, Berufs(sportler)*	Professional footballers earn a lot of money.
race	*Rennen*	Car races take place in Indianapolis.
racing	*(Pferde)Rennen*	The British like horse racing.
riding (to) ride	*Reiten* *reiten*	Jennifer is fond of riding.
rule	*Regel, Vorschrift*	Every game has its rules.

vocabulary	dt. Bedeutung	English sentence
runner	*Läufer(in)*	A marathon is a big event for runners.
(to) sail	*segeln*	Richard goes sailing in the summer.
score	*Punktestand*	What's the score?
skateboarding	*Skateboard fahren*	Many kids enjoy skateboarding.
skiing (to) ski	*Ski fahren*	We go skiing in Switzerland every winter.
soccer	*(europäischer) Fußball*	European football is also called soccer.
spectator	*Zuschauer(in)*	The new Wembley stadium has seats for 90,000 spectators.
sport	*Sport, Sportart*	What is your favorite sport?
sportsman	*Sportler(in)*	Joe is a very good sportsman.
stadium	*Stadion*	The new Wembley stadium is very modern.
(to) succeed	*Erfolg haben*	If you want to succeed, you have to train hard.
success	*Erfolg*	Success comes with hard work and fitness.
uccessful	*erfolgreich*	The player is successful because he trains a lot.
to) support	*unterstützen*	Good fans always support their team.
upporter	*Fan, (Fußball)Anhänger*	I am a supporter of Bayern Munich.
weat	*Schweiß*	In the changing rooms there is a smell of sweat in the air.
eam	*Mannschaft*	South Africa has the best rugby team.
icket	*Eintrittskarte*	Tickets for the final game are very expensive.
rack and field	*Leichtathletik*	Americans are good at track and field events.

vocabulary	dt. Bedeutung	English sentence
tracksuit	*Jogginganzug*	I would like a new tracksuit for Christmas.
(to) train	*trainieren*	Sportsmen have to train hard every day.
trainer	*Trainer(in)*	Our trainer does not like it when we are late.
trainers	*Turnschuhe*	I would like to have new trainers for my birthday.
victory	*Sieg*	Our team was very happy about the victory.
violence	*Gewalttätigkeit*	Real football fans don't like violence.
(to) watch sport on TV	*Sport im Fernsehen sehen*	My dad likes watching sport on TV.
(to) watch out	*aufpassen*	Watch out! The ball!
water sport	*Wassersport*	Canoeing is a popular water sport.
(to) work out	*trainieren*	My brother works out at the fitness centre.

Travelling and Transport

vocabulary	dt. Bedeutung	English sentence
abroad	*im, ins Ausland*	Have you ever been abroad?
accommodation	*Unterkunft*	Bed & Breakfasts in England offer cheap accommodation to tourists.
accident	*Unfall*	I saw a bad accident on my way to school.
adventure	*Abenteuer*	Our trip to the Scottish Highlands was a real adventure.
airport	*Flughafen*	We fly to Mallorca from Gatwick airport.
ambulance	*Notarztwagen, Ambulanz*	When I saw the accident I called the ambulance straight away.
arrival	*Ankunft*	At the airport follow the signs for "arrivals".
attraction	*Attraktion, Anziehungspunkt*	Disney World in Florida is a tourist attraction.
bike, bicycle	*Fahrrad*	I go to school by bike.
boarding pass	*Bordkarte*	You need a boarding pass to get onto the plane.
(to) ride a bike	*Fahrrad fahren*	Riding a bike keeps you fit.
(to) book	*reservieren, buchen*	My father always books our hotel rooms on the internet.
break	*Pause*	I am so tired – let's take a break!
(to) take a break	*eine Pause machen*	
breakdown	*Panne*	Last August our car had a break-down on the Kingston Bypass.
brochure	*Broschüre, Prospekt*	I like looking through holiday brochures.
by bus	*mit dem Bus*	Every morning many pupils get to school by bus.

vocabulary	dt. Bedeutung	English sentence
bus stop	*Bushaltestelle*	I was waiting at the bus stop for fifty minutes.
by rail	*mit der Bahn*	It is better to go by rail than by car.
camp-site	*Campingplatz*	My favourite camp-site is in Tintagel in Cornwall.
(to) cancel	*streichen, annulieren, absagen*	The flight was cancelled because of bad weather.
capital	*Hauptstadt*	London is the capital of Britain.
car (to) drive a car	*Auto* *Auto fahren*	When young people are 17 they can drive a car.
(to) change trains	*umsteigen*	When we travel to Pontypridd we must change trains in Cardiff.
Channel Tunnel	*der Ärmelkanaltunnel*	The Channel Tunnel is 49 kilometres long.
coach by coach	*Reisebus* *mit dem Bus*	The Smiths travel from London to Scotland by coach.
connection	*Verbindung*	The fastest connection between London and Paris is the Eurostar train.
congested	*überfüllt, verstopft*	The roads in the city of London are often congested.
(to) cost	*kosten*	How much does a train ticket to Glasgow cost?
continent	*Kontinent*	Australia is the fifth continent.
(to) cross	*überqueren*	We crossed the Channel at night.
crowded	*voll (mit Menschen)*	At weekends many trains are crowded with people.
delay (to) be delayed	*Verspätung* *Verspätung haben*	Our train was delayed by two hours.
(to) depart	*abfahren, abfliegen*	The trains to Oxford all depart from platform 7.

vocabulary	dt. Bedeutung	English sentence
departure	*Abflug, Abfahrt*	We arrived at the airport two hours before departure.
destination	*Reiseziel, Zielort*	New York is a favourite tourist destination.
direction	*Richtung*	The girls went into the other direction.
(to) discover	*entdecken*	When we walk through the city of London we always discover new things.
double-decker	*Doppeldecker-*	Everybody knows the red London double-decker busses.
driving licence	*Führerschein*	It's now possible to get a driving licence at the age of 17.
driving test	*Führerscheinprüfung*	Congratulations! You passed your driving test.
engine	*Maschine, Motor*	Our family car has a strong engine.
expensive	*teuer*	Running a car is very expensive today.
(to) explore	*erforschen*	The boys spent their afternoon exploring the town.
fast	*schnell*	Some young men drive much too fast.
(to) fasten	*festmachen*	Fasten your seatbelt, please.
ferry	*Fähre*	A ferry goes from Dover to Calais.
flight	*Flug*	Do you remember your first flight?
(to) go on a trip	*eine Reise machen*	Our class went on a trip to Nottingham.
(to) go sightseeing	*Sehenswürdigkeiten anschauen*	Tourists from all over the world go sightseeing in London.
guide (to) guide	*Reiseführer;* *leiten,führen*	A tourist guide shows us the city.

vocabulary	dt. Bedeutung	English sentence
inhabitant	*Einwohner(in)*	Great Britain has about 60 million inhabitants.
journey	*Reise*	Mr Henning went on a journey around the world.
known	*bekannt*	Windsor is known for its famous castle.
(to) land	*landen*	Every day hundreds of planes land in London Heathrow.
means of transport	*Verkehrsmittel*	The bicycle is a cheap means of transport.
mile	*Meile*	A mile is 1.6 kilometres.
motorway	*Autobahn*	People drive fast on the motorway.
narrow	*eng*	Some streets in the city centre are very narrow.
non-smoking	*Nichtraucher-*	All flights are non-smoking flights.
(to) operate	*verkehren, bedienen*	Connex trains operate in South London.
overcrowded	*überfüllt*	The early trains to London are often overcrowded.
(to) pack	*(zusammen)packen*	We pack our bags for a day out in the country.
(to) pass	*vorbeifahren, -gehen*	On our way to Wales we passed Windsor Castle.
passenger	*Passagier*	There were 265 passengers on the flight to Dublin.
passport	*(Reise)Pass*	When you travel to a foreign country you need to bring your passport.
peak time	*Hauptverkehrszeit*	Peak time in New York is called "rush hour".
petrol station	*Tankstelle*	You can buy drinks and get something to eat at a petrol station.

vocabulary	dt. Bedeutung	English sentence
platform	*Bahnsteig, Gleis*	The train to Edinburgh leaves from platform 14.
population	*Bevölkerung*	London has a population of about 7.5 million.
price **(to) go up in price**	*Preis* *im Preis steigen, teurer werden*	The London travel card has gone up in price.
quick	*schnell*	You can buy your ticket quickly from a vending machine ("Automat").
rail **(to) go off the rails**	*Schiene* *entgleisen*	The train went off the rails.
railway	*Eisenbahn*	The first railway ran between Liverpool and Manchester.
(to) reach	*erreichen*	We shall reach Birmingham in two hours.
ready **(to) get ready**	*fertig, bereit* *sich fertig machen*	The friends got ready for a picnic in the mountains.
reservation	*Reservierung*	Have you made your hotel reservation online?
(to) return	*zurückkommen*	My grandparents returned from their trip to Ireland.
ride **(to) go for a ride**	*Spazierfahrt* *eine Spazierfahrt machen*	Let's go for a ride to Brighton.
road	*(Land)Straße*	The road where we live is full of cars.
road works	*Straßenbauarbeiten*	Drive slowly! Road works ahead.
route	*Route, Strecke*	We worked out a route for our next bike tour.
(to) run out of sth.	*ausgehen, etwas nicht mehr haben*	My dad always makes sure that we do not run out of petrol.
rush hour	*Hauptverkehrszeit*	In the rush hour the busses are always full.

vocabulary	dt. Bedeutung	English sentence
(at the) seaside	*am Meer*	We spent our holidays at the seaside.
seasick	*seekrank*	When the boat moves I feel seasick.
seat	*(Sitz)Platz*	It's not easy to get a seat on the London Underground.
seatbelt	*Gurt*	Car passengers must wear seatbelts.
ship	*Schiff*	The Queen Mary is one of the largest ships today.
sights	*Sehenswürdigkeiten*	We visited all the sights in York.
speed	*Geschwindigkeit*	The train travels at a speed of 150 miles per hour.
speed limit	*Geschwindigkeits-beschränkung*	In the city the speed limit for cars is 30 miles.
(to) study a map	*eine Karte studieren*	My mother always studies the map before we go on holiday.
subway	[BE] *Unterführung* [AE] *U-Bahn*	Use a subway to cross a busy road safely. The New York subway takes you quickly from one stop to the next.
(to) be stuck	*stecken bleiben*	In London we got stuck in a traffic jam.
(to) take off	*starten*	Our plane takes off at 9 o'clock.
ticket	*Fahrkarte, Ticket*	I buy my train ticket from a vending machine ("Automat").
timetable	*Fahrplan*	The new timetable has not changed much.
together	*zusammen*	We always go on holiday together with my aunt and uncle.
tour (of)	*Reise*	I would like to go on a tour of Canada.
tourist	*Tourist(in)*	London is always full of tourists.
traffic	*Verkehr*	Traffic on roads is dangerous.

vocabulary	dt. Bedeutung	English sentence
traffic jam	*Verkehrsstau*	There is always a traffic jam on the M 25.
traffic lights	*Verkehrsampel*	You must stop when the traffic lights are red.
train	*Zug*	The last train to Glasgow leaves at 11 o'clock at night.
tram	*Straßenbahn*	Not many cities still have trams.
transport	*Verkehr*	London has a good transport system.
(to) travel	*reisen*	When I'm older I'll travel round the world.
travel agency	*Reisebüro*	We always book our holidays at our local travel agency.
trip (to)	*Reise (nach)*	Mrs Hills won on a trip to Cornwall.
(to) go on a trip	*einen Ausflug machen*	Leo's class is going on a trip to Chessington Zoo.
tube	*U-Bahn*	We take the tube to Charing Cross.
underground	*Untergrund; U-Bahn*	Most tourists go on the London Underground.
vacation	*Ferien*	"Vacation" is the American word for "holiday".
(to) wait	*warten*	At the London Eye tourists often wait for hours.
weather forecast	*Wettervorhersage, Wetterbericht*	What does the weather forecast say?
youth hostel	*Jugendherberge*	We stay at a youth hostel because it's cheap.

World of Work

vocabulary	dt. Bedeutung	English sentence
abroad	*im/ins Ausland*	My brother Luke works abroad in Australia.
ad, advert (= advertise-ment)	*Anzeige, Reklame*	Don't you think there are too many ads on TV?
address	*Adresse*	We moved houses in summer, so our address has changed.
(to) advertise	*werben*	Firms advertise for their new products.
advice	*Rat(schlag)*	Please listen to my advice.
(to) advise	*jdm. etwas raten*	An expert can advise you if you don't know what to do after school.
agency	*Agentur*	Susan works in a travel agency.
aim	*Ziel*	What is your aim in life?
almost	*fast, beinahe*	Wait, I'm almost done!
ambitious	*ehrgeizig*	Ambitious people work a lot more than others.
application	*Bewerbung*	Marks & Spencer are looking for new shop assistants. Why not send an application?
(to) apply	*sich bewerben*	Marion applies for a job at a bank.
apprentice	*Auszubildende(r), Lehrling*	An apprentice doesn't earn much money.
apprenticeship	*Berufsausbildung, Lehre*	Ralph wants to start an apprenticeship as a carpenter.
artist	*Künstler(in)*	Julian is a graffiti artist.
(to) attend	*besuchen, teilnehmen an*	Kate attends Greenford Comprehensive School.
au pair (girl)	*Au-pair-Mädchen*	Beatrice work as an au pair in Paris.

vocabulary	dt. Bedeutung	English sentence
(to) be employed	*angestellt sein*	My uncle is employed in a bank in Glasgow.
between	*zwischen*	The shop closes between 12 and 2 o'clock.
boss	*Chef(in)*	Being a boss is not always an easy job.
branch	*hier: Filiale*	There is a branch of the NatWest Bank near to where we live.
business	*Geschäft; Firma*	Dave is interested in a job in the music business.
career	*(berufliche) Laufbahn*	Many boys dream of a big career in football.
careers adviser	*Berufsberater(in)*	Benny's careers adviser suggested the job of travel agent.
carpenter	*Tischler(in), Zimmerer(in)*	A carpenter makes wooden tables and chairs.
chance	*Chance, Möglichkeit*	You have a good chance of finding a job when you pass your exams.
colleague	*Kollege, Kollegin*	My mother says her colleagues at work are very helpful.
company	*Firma*	Microsoft is a successful computer company.
(to) compete	*konkurrieren, im Wettbewerb stehen*	British firms compete with US and German firms.
(to) complain	*sich beschweren, beklagen*	The neighbours complained about the smoke from the factory.
(to) concentrate	*sich konzentrieren*	I cannot concentrate when you play loud music.
confused	*verwirrt, durcheinander*	Britney looked confused when she saw what she had to do.
(to) consume	*verbrauchen*	We consume too much energy.
contract	*Vertrag*	My father's work contract runs out next year.

vocabulary	dt. Bedeutung	English sentence
customer	*Kunde, Kundin*	Mr Craig is a regular customer in the corner shop.
CV (curriculum vitae)	*Lebenslauf*	When you apply for a job you have to send an up-to-date CV.
Dear Sir or Madam	*Sehr geehrte Damen und Herren*	A business letter normally begins with "Dear Sir or Madam".
(to) decide	*sich entscheiden*	Before you leave school you have to decide what job you want to do.
decision	*Entscheidung*	It was a good decision to learn Spanish.
department	*Abteilung*	Twenty-five people work in the firm's computer department.
department store	*Kaufhaus*	Harrods is a big department store in London.
diary	*Terminkalender*	The secretary keeps a diary for her boss.
during	*während*	During the Christmas holidays the firm is closed.
(to) earn	*verdienen*	Footballers earn a lot.
(to) earn a living	*seinen Lebensunterhalt verdienen*	Can you really earn a living by giving music lessons?
easy	*leicht*	Starting a new job is not always easy.
engineering	*Technik; Maschinenbau*	My cousin Paul studies engineering in Nottingham.
exactly	*genau*	Every morning our neighbour Wilbur leaves for work at exactly half past six.
experience	*Erfahrung*	Working for a week or two during the holidays is a good experience for pupils.
factory	*Fabrik*	The factory where my uncle Jeff works will close down soon.
(to) finish	*beenden*	Have you finished your project?

vocabulary	dt. Bedeutung	English sentence
firm	*Firma*	Harry Paul started his own firm in January.
foreign	*ausländisch*	Dave Windermere works for a foreign company.
(to) forget	*vergessen*	Don't forget to finish your project soon.
full-time	*Vollzeit*	Mrs Muir worked full-time until she had her children.
(to) get on	*auskommen, sich verstehen*	My dad gets on very well with his boss.
(to) give up	*aufgeben*	Susan gave up her job at the fast food restaurant.
global	*global, weltweit*	We live in a global economy ("Wirtschaft").
globe	*Globus, Erdball*	Coca Cola is sold around the globe.
goods	*Ware*	British firms export their goods to many countries.
holiday	*Ferien, Urlaub*	At the moment we are on holiday in Italy.
holiday job	*Ferienjob*	A holiday job is a good possibility to earn some money.
hour	*Stunde*	Many people work 35 hours a week.
improvement	*Verbesserung*	Mobile phones are a great improvement and make life much easier.
industrial	*industriell*	The Industrial Revolution began in England.
industry	*Industrie*	My uncle started work in the car industry in 1980.
(to) inform	*informieren*	This magazine informs about jobs in the European Union.
(to) interrupt	*unterbrechen*	I interrupted my work to talk to Sally on the phone.

vocabulary	dt. Bedeutung	English sentence
job	*Arbeit, Tätigkeit, Aufgabe*	Alwyn is looking for a new job.
kind	*nett, freundlich*	Would you be so kind and open the window?
knowledge	*Wissen, Kenntnisse*	A good knowledge of foreign languages is necessary for most jobs.
letter of application	*Bewerbungsschreiben*	My brother sent a letter of application to the Royal Bank of Scotland.
mainly	*hauptsächlich*	Microsoft makes mainly computer programmes.
manager	*Geschäftsführer(in)*	Mr Greenwood is the manager of a big hotel.
market	*Markt*	Mrs Cohen sells fruit in the market.
material	*Material*	Nylon is a strong material.
money	*Geld*	Everybody would like to earn good money.
nowadays	*heutzutage*	Banks cannot work without computers nowadays.
(to) offer	*anbieten*	Many firms offer holiday jobs for students.
office	*Büro*	Thirty people work in Mr Henning's office.
office hours	*Bürozeiten*	Office hours are usually from 9 am to 5 pm.
on time	*pünktlich*	I get up early because I want to be on time.
open	*offen*	In the States big supermarkets are open 24 hours a day.
opening hours	*Öffnungszeiten*	Next week the supermarket will have new opening hours.
part-time	*Teilzeit*	Many mothers work part-time.

vocabulary	dt. Bedeutung	English sentence
(to) pay (for)	*bezahlen*	I paid for the trip with my own pocket money.
pay	*Bezahlung*	The pay in the car industry is quite good.
pay rise	*Gehaltserhöhung*	The secretary asked for a pay rise.
(to) phone	*anrufen*	My sister Karen phones her friend Stella four or five times a day.
(to) photocopy	*fotokopieren*	Could you photocopy this page for me?
possible	*möglich*	Is it possible to start a language course next month?
practical	*praktisch*	Kevin can walk to work, which is very practical.
(to) prefer	*vorziehen*	Many girls prefer working in an office to a factory.
project	*Vorhaben*	At school we are working on a project about the rain forests.
(to) protect	*schützen*	Building workers protect their heads with a hard hat ("Helm").
proud	*stolz*	Graham is very proud that he works for an international company.
quite	*ziemlich*	My dad's job is quite important.
reason	*Grund*	The main reason why people went to America was for a better life.
regular	*regelmäßig*	For most people a regular income ("Einkommen") is important.
salary	*Gehalt*	She gets a salary of £ 50,000 a year.
sale	*Verkauf*	The noun that goes with "to sell" is "sale".
for sale	*zu verkaufen*	Our house is for sale.
sales	*Schlussverkauf, Verkauf; Vertrieb*	I bought his jumper in the sales.

vocabulary	dt. Bedeutung	English sentence
school leaver	*Schulabgänger(in)*	Many school leavers do not know what job they want to do.
secretary	*Sekretär(in)*	My dad's secretary is called Miss Stevens.
(to) sell	*verkaufen*	Selling songs through the Internet has become a big business.
shop assistant	*Verkäufer(in)*	Being a shop assistant in a shoe shop is many girls' dream.
(to) suggest	*vorschlagen*	Can you suggest a good holiday job?
suggestion	*Vorschlag*	I don't like that suggestion.
trade	*Handel*	London is the centre of international trade.
trade fair	*Messe*	People from all over the world come to the trade fair in Frankfurt.
(to) train	*eine Ausbildung machen*	Peter trains as a cook.
trainee	*Auszubildende(r)*	Harold is "trainee of the month" in the fast food restaurant.
trainer	*Ausbilder(in)*	Harold's trainer is very strict.
training	*Ausbildung*	Steve begins his training for a job next Monday.
(to) be used to	*gewöhnt sein*	My grandmother was used to working hard in the garden.
wage	*Lohn*	Wages for people who work in fast food restaurants are low.
waiter	*Bedienung, Kellner*	A waiter is working when other people enjoy their free time.
waitress	*weibliche Bedienung*	Sophie wants to be a waitress.
(to) be out of work	*arbeitslos sein*	My poor uncle. He's been out of work for six months now.
workshop	*Werkstatt*	My granddad spends hours in his workshop.

Computer and Media

vocabulary	dt. Bedeutung	English sentence
advantage	*Vorteil*	What are the advantages of a computer?
(to) afford	*sich leisten*	Children cannot afford to buy expensive play stations.
all over the world	*auf der ganzen Welt*	All over the world people use the internet.
article	*Artikel*	Laura writes an article for the school magazine.
basic	*grundlegend, grundsätzlich*	Most kids have basic computer knowledge.
(to) browse	*blättern, schmökern, durchstöbern*	I often browse the BBC web pages.
button	*Knopf, Taste*	You have to press the "play" button.
(to) buy	*kaufen*	I think people buy too much today.
calculator	*Taschenrechner*	My dad uses a calculator to add up sums.
(to) carry out	*ausführen*	A computer carries out orders.
channel	*Kanal, Fernsehprogramm*	I think there are too many TV channels.
(to) chat	*sich unterhalten*	Chatting on the internet has become very popular.
(to) check	*überprüfen*	I check my email regularly.
chat room	*Chatroom (im Internet)*	Jeff met his girlfriend Susan in a chat room.
(to) click	*klicken*	You have to click your mouse twice.
(to) close	*schließen*	When I finish work I close down the programme.
(to) communicate	*kommunizieren, Nachrichten austauschen*	In chat rooms we can now communicate electronically.

vocabulary	dt. Bedeutung	English sentence
communication	*Kommunikation*	E-Mail communication is quicker than writing letters.
(to) connect	*verbinden*	All the PCs here are connected to a central computer.
connection	*Verbindung*	To surf the internet you need a fast connection.
(to) contact	*Kontakt aufnehmen mit, sich wenden an*	If you wish to contact us, please send us an email.
(to) design	*entwerfen, gestalten*	This company designs web sites.
designer	*Layouter(in), Gestalter(in)*	Helen works as a designer.
disk drive	*Diskettenlaufwerk*	My computer has two disk drives.
(to) download	*herunterladen*	I download the new version of the game from the internet.
(to) draw	*zeichnen*	You can draw pictures with a computer programme.
DVD burner	*DVD-Brenner*	When you have a DVD burner you can save lots of data on a DVD.
DVD drive	*DVD-Laufwerk*	All computers have a DVD drive today.
(to) edit	*bearbeiten, redigieren*	James edits a webpage before he puts it on the internet.
email	*electronic mail, (elektronische Post), Email*	Please send us an email.
(to) exit	*verlassen, beenden*	When you have finished work exit the programme.
expensive	*teuer*	Video games are often expensive.
experience	*Erfahrung*	Surfing the internet is an interesting experience.
expert	*Fachmann, Experte, Expertin*	Are you a computer expert?

vocabulary	dt. Bedeutung	English sentence
(to) explain	*erklären*	Can you explain how a computer works?
fast	*schnell*	Broadband ("DSL") is a fast internet connection.
fee	*Gebühr*	To use the service you have to pay a fee.
file	*Datei*	You save files on your hard disk.
(to) find	*finden*	You can find lots of information on the internet.
future	*Zukunft*	In future we will become more dependent on computers.
global	*global, weltweit*	The internet is a global experience.
grown-up	*Erwachsene(r)*	Many grown-ups think that kids play on their computers too much.
hard disk	*Festplatte*	My hard disk is almost full; I must buy a bigger one.
harmful	*schädlich*	A computer virus is harmful.
(to) have got	*haben*	How many computers have you got in your house?
(to) have to	*müssen*	I have to stop now; it is late.
headline	*Schlagzeile*	I always read the headlines of our newspaper.
nternet **on the internet**	*im Internet*	You can find a lot of information on the internet.
nvention	*Erfindung*	The computer is a wonderful invention.
T (information technology)	*IT, Informatik*	My brother studies information technology.
ournalist	*Journalist(in)*	*The Times* offers jobs to the best journalists.
keyboard	*Tastatur*	I like my new keyboard.

vocabulary	dt. Bedeutung	English sentence
knowledge	*Wissen, Kenntnis(se)*	Computer knowledge is important today.
language	*Sprache*	Most computer programmes come in different languages.
latest	*das neueste*	Do have the latest version of the programme?
(to) listen	*hören*	I listen to the news on the radio.
(to) listen to the radio	*Radio hören*	My granddad does not watch TV much; he likes listening to the radio.
(to) load	*laden*	If you want to work with a programme, you have to load it first.
(to) log in	*einloggen*	At his office my father logs into his computer every morning.
(to) log on	*sich anmelden, sich einwählen*	On many web sites you have to log on first.
(to) look up	*nachschlagen*	I often look up words I don't know in an online dictionary.
lots of	*jede Menge*	Marc has lots of CDs and DVDs.
magazine	*Zeitschrift*	*Teen* is a very popular magazine for young girls.
magic	*Zauber, Magie*	Some older people think that computers are like magic.
means of communication	*Kommunikationsmittel*	The Internet is an important means of communication.
message	*Nachricht, Botschaft*	Jane sends messages to all her friends.
monitor	*Bildschirm*	I would like a bigger monitor, mine is too small.
mouse	*Maus*	A computer mouse does not run away.
nervous	*nervös*	My mum says computers make her nervous.

ocabulary	dt. Bedeutung	English sentence
et	*das Netz, Internet*	Millions surf the net every day.
ews	*Nachricht*	On the internet you can read the latest news.
ewspaper	*Zeitung*	Our neighbour reads three newspapers every day.
n TV	*im Fernsehen*	My dad always watches the news on TV.
pinion	*Meinung*	What is your opinion on video games for children?
rder	*Befehl*	Computers carry out orders.
to) organise	*einrichten, ordnen, gliedern*	You have to organise your files if you want to find things quickly.
wn	*eigen(e)*	Many people have their own web site.
to) own	*besitzen*	How many video games do you own?
wner	*Besitzer(in)*	Mr Patel is the owner of an internet café.
age	*Seite*	Most newspapers have a page with the TV programmes.
aper	*Papier*	I get some pen and paper and write to my grandparents.
aper (= newspaper)	*Zeitung*	My mum reads the paper every morning at breakfast.
icture	*Bild*	Newspapers are full of pictures today.
opular	*beliebt*	Surfing the net is a popular pastime ("Freizeitbeschäftigung").
ractice	*Übung*	Practice makes perfect.
o) practise	*üben*	The more you practise the better you get.

vocabulary	dt. Bedeutung	English sentence
(to) print	*drucken*	Could you print this page for me, please?
printer	*Drucker*	At my dad's work they have three laser printers.
printout	*Ausdruck*	A printout is a paper with information printed on it.
radio on the radio	*Radio*	I heard it on the radio.
(to) repeat	*wiederholen*	Please repeat what you said; I didn't hear you.
(to) report (on)	*berichten (über)*	The newspapers report on international football matches.
report	*Bericht*	I watched a report on "Computers in the classroom".
reporter	*Reporter(in)*	The film star spoke to the reporters about her new film.
research	*Forschung, Nachforschung*	Tim has to do some research on the internet.
result	*Ergebnis*	What was the result of your internet search?
role	*Rolle*	Newspapers play an important role for many people.
safe	*sicher*	Is your computer safe?
(to) save	*speichern*	Do not forget to save your work.
screen	*Bildschirm*	People like to see films on the big screen.
(to) search	*suchen*	Before we go on holiday my dad searches on the Internet for a good campsite.
search engine	*Suchmaschine*	Google and Yahoo are search engines.
(to) send	*senden*	I must send an e-card to my friend Gregory; it's his birthday tomorrow.

vocabulary	dt. Bedeutung	English sentence
short	*kurz*	Emails must be short; nobody wants to read long texts.
simple	*einfach*	Using a computer is not difficult; most people find it simple.
site	*hier: Seite*	There are millions of interesting sites on the net.
size	*Größe*	Hard disks have become bigger in size.
skill	*Fähigkeit, Fertigkeit*	Computer skills are important today.
slow	*langsam*	My PC is too slow.
SMS (short message service)	*SMS, Kurznachricht*	Young people use SMS more often than email.
software programme	*Computerprogramm*	Bill Gates was young when he wrote his first software programme.
spelling mistake	*Rechtschreibfehler*	My dad says that there are too many spelling mistakes in our emails.
(to) spend money (on)	*Geld ausgeben (für)*	Teenagers spend a lot of money on computer games.
(to) store	*speichern*	A computer can store a lot of information.
to) surf	*surfen*	Ray surfs the internet for hours every day.
to) switch off	*ausschalten*	Marc finds it hard to switch off his computer.
to) switch on	*einschalten*	As soon as he gets up Simon switches on his computer.
to) take pictures	*Fotos machen*	I take pictures for our school magazine.
to) talk	*sprechen*	Marc and Lena talk to each other over the internet.
echnical	*technisch, technologisch*	My older brother helps me with any technical problems.

vocabulary	dt. Bedeutung	English sentence
technology	*Technik*	Young people are interested in new technology.
(to) text	*eine SMS senden*	Please text us what you think about our programme.
text message	*SMS*	Many people write text messages more often than letters.
(to) turn off	*abschalten*	When I do my homework I turn off the radio.
(to) turn on	*einschalten*	When my mother works in the kitchen she turns on the radio.
TV	*Fernseher, Fernsehen*	Every evening at seven Mrs Shivers turns on her TV to watch the news.
(to) type in	*eintippen*	To start the programme you have to type in your name.
(to) understand	*verstehen*	My granddad does not understand why I like computer games.
(to) warn	*warnen*	My mum warns me about the dangers of the internet.
(to) waste	*verschwenden*	"Don't waste too much time playing games on the internet," my mum always says.
waste of time	*Zeitverschwendung*	Many people think that surfing the net is a waste of time.
(to) watch TV	*fernsehen*	My grandparents watch TV in the afternoon.
web site	*Seite im Internet*	Our school has its own web site.

Unregelmäßige Verben

Infinitive	Past Tense	Past Participle	deutsche Übersetzung
be	was	been	*sein*
beat	beat	beaten	*schlagen*
become	became	become	*werden*
begin	began	begun	*beginnen*
bend	bent	bent	*biegen*
bet	bet	bet	*wetten*
blow	blew	blown	*blasen*
break	broke	broken	*brechen*
bring	brought	brought	*bringen*
build	built	built	*bauen*
burn	burnt/ed	burnt/ed	*brennen*
buy	bought	bought	*kaufen*
catch	caught	caught	*fangen*
choose	chose	chosen	*wählen*
come	came	come	*kommen*
cost	cost	cost	*kosten*
cut	cut	cut	*schneiden*
do	did	done	*tun*
draw	drew	drawn	*zeichnen, ziehen*
dream	dreamt/ed	dreamt/ed	*träumen*
drink	drank	drunk	*trinken*
drive	drove	driven	*fahren*
eat	ate	eaten	*essen*
fall	fell	fallen	*fallen*
feed	fed	fed	*füttern*

Infinitive	Past Tense	Past Participle	deutsche Übersetzung
feel	felt	felt	*fühlen*
fight	fought	fought	*kämpfen*
find	found	found	*finden*
fit	fit/fitted	fit/fitted	*sich eignen, passen*
fly	flew	flown	*fliegen*
forget	forgot	forgotten	*vergessen*
get	got	got	*bekommen*
give	gave	given	*geben*
go	went	gone	*gehen*
grow	grew	grown	*wachsen*
hang	hung	hung	*hängen*
have	had	had	*haben*
hear	heard	heard	*hören*
hide	hid	hidden	*verbergen, (sich) verstecken*
hit	hit	hit	*treffen, schlagen*
hold	held	held	*halten*
hurt	hurt	hurt	*verletzen*
keep	kept	kept	*halten*
know	knew	known	*wissen*
lay	laid	laid	*legen*
lead	led	led	*leiten*
learn	learnt/ed	learnt/ed	*lernen*
leave	left	left	*lassen*
lend	lent	lent	*leihen*
lean	leant/ed	leant/ed	*lehnen*
let	let	let	*lassen*
lie	lay	lain	*liegen*
lose	lost	lost	*verlieren*

nfinitive	Past Tense	Past Participle	deutsche Übersetzung
nake	made	made	*machen*
nean	meant	meant	*meinen, bedeuten*
neet	met	met	*treffen*
vertake	overtook	overtaken	*überholen*
ay	paid	paid	*bezahlen*
ut	put	put	*setzen, stellen, legen*
ead	read	read	*lesen*
ebuild	rebuilt	rebuilt	*wieder aufbauen*
ide	rode	ridden	*fahren, reiten*
ing	rang	rung	*läuten*
un	ran	run	*laufen, rennen*
ay	said	said	*sagen*
ee	saw	seen	*sehen*
ell	sold	sold	*verkaufen*
end	sent	sent	*senden*
et up	set up	set up	*aufschlagen*
hake	shook	shaken	*schütteln*
hine	shone	shone	*scheinen*
hoot	shot	shot	*schießen*
how	showed	shown	*zeigen*
hut	shut	shut	*schließen*
ing	sang	sung	*singen*
t	sat	sat	*sitzen*
eep	slept	slept	*schlafen*
mell	smelt	smelt	*riechen*
peak	spoke	spoken	*sprechen*
pell	spelt/spelled	spelt/spelled	*buchstabieren*
pend	spent	spent	*verbringen, ausgeben*

Infinitive	Past Tense	Past Participle	deutsche Übersetzung
split	split	split	*spalten, teilen*
spoil	spoilt/ed	spoilt/ed	*verderben*
spring	sprang	sprung	*springen*
stand	stood	stood	*stehen*
steal	stole	stolen	*stehlen*
stick	stuck	stuck	*kleben*
sweep	swept	swept	*kehren, fegen*
swim	swam	swum	*schwimmen*
take	took	taken	*nehmen*
teach	taught	taught	*lehren*
tear	tore	torn	*reißen*
tell	told	told	*erzählen*
think	thought	thought	*denken, glauben*
throw	threw	thrown	*werfen*
tread	trod	trodden	*treten*
understand	understood	understood	*verstehen*
wake up	woke up	woken up	*aufwachen*
wear	wore	worn	*tragen*
win	won	won	*gewinnen*
write	wrote	written	*schreiben*

Alphabetischer Grundwortschatz

ability	*Fähigkeit*
able	*etwas tun können, fähig sein*
about	*über, ungefähr*
above	*über, oberhalb*
abroad	*ins, im Ausland*
absence	*Abwesenheit*
absolutely	*völlig, absolut*
accent	*Akzent*
(to) accept	*annehmen*
acceptable	*annehmbar, hinnehmbar*
accident	*Unfall*
accidental	*versehentlich, unbeabsichtigt*
accidentally	*versehentlich*
accommodation	*Unterkunft*
(to) accompany	*begleiten*
ccording	*gemäß, nach, entsprechend*
ccount	*Bericht; Konto*
(to) achieve	*etwas erreichen*
chievement	*Leistung*
cid rain	*saurer Regen*
cross	*über (… hinweg)*
(to) act	*handeln, sich verhalten*
ction	*Handeln*
active	*aktiv, lebhaft*
activity	*Tätigkeit, Beschäftigung*
actual	*eigentlich, tatsächlich*
actually	*eigentlich*
(to) adapt	*anpassen*
(to) add	*zusammenzählen, hinzufügen*
(to) adress	*ansprechen*
(to) admire	*bewundern*
admission	*Eintritt*
(to) admit	*zugeben*
(to) adopt	*adoptieren, Patenschaft übernehmen*
(to) advance	*vorrücken*
advantage	*Vorteil*
adventure	*Abenteuer*
(to) advertise	*werben für*
advertisement	*(Zeitungs)Anzeige, Reklame*
advertising	*Werbung, Reklame*
advice	*Rat(schlag)*
(to) advise	*beraten, jdm. raten*
(to) affect	*sich auswirken auf, (Gesundheit) angreifen*
(to) afford	*sich leisten*
afraid	*verängstigt*

after	*nach*
afternoon	*Nachmittag*
afterwards	*nachher, hinterher*
again	*wieder, noch einmal*
against	*gegen*
age	*Alter*
ago	*vor (… Jahren)*
(to) agree	*übereinstimmen*
agrement	*Vereinbarung*
ahead	*vorn, in Führung*
(to) aim	*zielen; Ziel*
air	*Luft*
airport	*Flughafen*
A-levels	*Abitur*
album	*Album*
alcohol	*Alkohol*
alive	*lebendig, (noch am Leben)*
all	*alle, alles*
(to) allow	*erlauben, ermöglichen*
almost	*fast, beinah*
alone	*allein*
along	*vorwärts*
already	*schon, bereits*
also	*auch, ebenfalls, außerdem*
although	*obwohl, obgleich*
always	*immer, ständig*
amazing	*erstaunlich*
ambulance	*Krankenwagen*
among	*unter, untereinander*
amount	*Betrag, Menge*
anger	*Zorn*
angry	*zornig*
animal	*Tier*
(to) announce	*ankündigen, bekannt geben*
another	*ein(e) andere(r, s), weiterer*
answer	*Antwort*
anxious	*gespannt*
any	*irgendein(e) beliebige(r,s)*
anybody	*jemand*
anyhow	*sowieso*
anyone	*jede(r)*
anything	*alles*
anyway	*jedenfalls, sowieso, immerhin*
anywhere	*überall*
apart	*getrennt, für sich*
apartment	*Wohnung*
(to) apologize	*sich entschuldigen*
(to) appeal	*jdn. reizen, jdm. gefallen*
(to) appear	*erscheinen*
appearance	*Erscheinung; Erscheinen, Aufkommen*
application	*Bewerbung*
(to) apply for	*sich bewerben um*

apprentice	*Lehrling, Auszubildende(r)*
(to) approve	*billigen*
area	*Gebiet, Bereich*
(to) argue	*argumentieren, sich aussprechen für*
(to) argue	*sich streiten*
argument	*Argument, Begründung; Streit*
arm	*Arm*
around	*um … herum*
(to) arrange	*vereinbaren*
arrangement	*Vereinbarung, Anordnung; Vorkehrung*
arrival	*Ankunft*
(to) arrive	*ankommen*
art	*(bildende) Kunst*
artificial	*künstlich, Kunst-*
as far as	*so weit*
ashamed	*beschämt*
(to) ask	*fragen*
(to) ask for	*bitten*
assistant	*Assistent(in), Gehilfe / Gehilfin, Verkäufer(in)*
at last	*endlich*
at least	*wenigstens*
at night	*nachts*
at school	*in der Schule*
(to) attach	*etwas befestigen; verbinden, beilegen*
(to) attempt	*versuchen, Versuch*
(to) attend	*etwas besuchen, anwesend sein*
attention	*Aufmerksamkeit, Beachtung*
attitude	*Haltung, Einstellung*
(to) attract	*anziehen*
attraction	*Attraktion, Sehenswürdigkeit*
attractive	*attraktiv, anziehend*
audience	*Zuschauer, Publikum*
author	*Autor(in)*
automatic	*automatisch*
autumn	*Herbst*
available	*erhältlich, verfügbar*
average	*Durchschnitt*
(to) avoid	*vermeiden*
(to) awake	*aufwachen, erwachen*
aware	*bewusst*
away	*weg*
back	*zurück*
backward	*rückwärts gewandt*
bad	*schlecht, schlimm*
badly	*schlecht; sehr, dringend*
bag	*Tasche*
baggage [AE]	*Gepäck*
balance	*Gleichgewicht*
balanced	*ausgeglichen*
bald	*kahl*

banana	*Banane*
band	*Band, Gruppe*
bang	*Knall*
bank	*Bank; Ufer*
bar	*Stange; Riegel*
barbecue	*Grillparty*
bare	*bloß, nackt*
base	*Sockel, Basis*
basic	*grundlegend, fundamental, einfach*
basically	*im Wesentlichen, im Grunde*
basis	*Grundlage, Basis*
basket	*Korb*
bat	*Schläger*
bath	*(Bade)Wanne, Bad*
bathroom	*Badezimmer*
battery	*Batterie*
battle	*Schlacht*
(to) be able to	*können*
(to) be going to	*werden*
(to) be in love with	*lieben, verliebt sein in*
beach	*Strand*
bear	*Bär*
(to) bear	*ertragen*
(to) beat	*schlagen; besiegen*
beautiful	*schön*
because	*weil*
because of	*wegen*
(to) become	*werden*
bed	*Bett*
bedroom	*Schlafzimmer*
beef	*Rindfleisch*
beer	*Bier*
before	*vor*
(to) begin	*anfangen*
(to) behave	*sich benehmen*
behaviour	*Verhalten, Benehmen*
behind	*hinten, dahinter, zurück*
belief	*Glaube, Überzeugung*
(to) believe in	*glauben an*
(to) belong to	*angehören, Mitglied sein in*
below	*unten, unter*
belt	*Gürtel*
bench	*(Park, Garten)Bank*
bend	*Kurve*
(to) bend down	*sich bücken*
benefit	*Nutzen, Vorteil*
beside	*neben*
besides	*außer*
(to) bet	*wetten; Wette*
best	*(der/die/das) beste*
better	*besser*
between	*zwischen*
beyond	*jenseits, darüber hinaus*
bicycle	*Fahrrad*

big	*groß*
bike	*Fahrrad*
bill	*Rechnung, Banknote*
bin	*Mülleimer*
biology	*Biologie*
bird	*Vogel*
biro	*Kugelschreiber*
birth	*Geburt*
birthday	*Geburtstag*
bit	*Stückchen, Stück*
(to) bite	*beißen; Biss*
black	*schwarz*
(to) blame	*die Schuld geben, beschuldigen; Schuld*
blanket	*Decke*
blind	*blind*
block	*Block, Holzklotz*
block of flats	*Wohnhaus, Mietshaus*
blonde	*blond*
blood	*Blut*
blouse	*Bluse*
(to) blow	*wehen, blasen*
blue	*blau; traurig, deprimiert*
(to) blush	*rot werden*
board	*Brett, Tafel*
boarding pass	*Bordkarte*
boat	*Boot, Schiff*
body	*Körper*
(to) boil	*kochen, abkochen*
bone	*Knochen*
book	*Buch*
booking	*Reservierung*
bookshelf	*Bücherregal*
bookshop	*Buchhandlung*
border	*Grenze*
bored	*gelangweilt*
boring	*langweilig*
born	*geboren*
borough	*Stadtbezirk*
(to) borrow	*borgen, sich ausleihen*
boss	*Chef(in)*
both	*beide*
(to) bother	*jdn. belästigen*
bottle	*Flasche*
bottom	*Grund, unterster Teil, Boden*
bowl	*Schale, Schüssel, Napf*
box	*Kiste*
boy	*Junge*
boyfriend	*Freund*
brain	*Gehirn, Verstand, Intelligenz*
(to) brake	*bremsen; Bremse*
branch	*Zweig; Filiale, Zweigstelle*
brave	*tapfer, mutig*
bread	*Brot*

breadth	*Breite, Weite*
break	*Pause*
(to) break	*brechen*
(to) break up	*zerbrechen, auseinander gehen*
breakfast	*Frühstück*
breath	*Atem*
(to) breathe	*atmen*
bride	*Braut*
bridegroom	*Bräutigam*
bridge	*Brücke*
brief	*kurz, bündig*
bright	*hell*
(to) bring up	*aufziehen, großziehen*
broad	*breit, weit*
(to) broadcast	*senden, übertragen (TV)*
brochure	*Broschüre, Prospekt*
broken	*zerbrochen*
brother	*Bruder*
brown	*braun*
(to) brush	*bürsten, putzen; Bürste*
budgie	*Wellensittich*
(to) build	*bauen*
building	*Gebäude*
bunch	*Büschel; (Blumen)Strauß*
burden	*Last*
(to) burn	*brennen, verbrennen*
(to) burst	*brechen*
(to) bury	*begraben*
bus	*Omnibus, Schulbus*
bush	*Busch, Gebüsch*
business	*Unternehmen, Geschäft, Branche*
business woman	*Geschäftsfrau, Unternehmerin*
businessman	*Unternehmer, Geschäftsmann*
busy	*belebt, beschäftigt*
but	*aber*
butter	*Butter*
button	*Knopf*
(to) buy	*kaufen*
by birth	*von Geburt*
by mistake	*aus Versehen*
by trade	*von Beruf*
bye-bye	*Auf Wiedersehen*
cable	*Kabel*
café	*Café, kleines Restaurant*
cafeteria	*Kantine, Selbstbedienungsrestaurant*
cage	*Käfig*
cake	*Kuchen, Torte*
calendar	*Kalender*
(to) call	*rufen, nennen; Anruf*
calm	*ruhig, gelassen*
camera	*Kamera*

camp	*(Trainings, Zelt)Lager*
camp-site	*Campingsplatz*
can	*können*
can [AE]	*Büchse, Dose*
(to) cancel	*annullieren, streichen, absagen*
candle	*Kerze*
canteen	*Kantine*
canyon	*Schlucht*
cap	*Mütze*
capital	*Hauptstadt*
captain	*Kapitän*
caption	*Bildunterschrift*
car	*Wagen*
card	*Karte*
cardboard	*Pappe*
(to) care	*sich kümmern, sorgen für; Sorgfalt*
career	*Karriere, Laufbahn*
careful	*vorsichtig*
careless	*unvorsichtig*
carpenter	*Zimmermann*
carriage	*Wagen, (Zug)Waggon*
(to) carry	*tragen*
carton	*Karton, (Milch, Saft)Packung*
case	*Fall*
cash	*Bargeld*
(to) cash	*einlösen; Bargeld*
cassette	*Kassette*
cassette recorder	*Kassettenrekorder*
castle	*Schloss*
cat	*Katze*
(to) catch	*fangen, ergreifen*
cathedral	*Kathedrale, Dom*
cause	*Grund, Anlass*
(to) celebrate	*feiern*
celebration	*Feier*
centimetre	*Zentimeter*
central	*Zentral-, Mittel-*
centre	*Mitte, Zentrum*
century	*Jahrhundert*
cereal	*Getreide, Getreideflocken*
certain	*sicher, gewiss*
certainly	*sicherlich, gewiss*
chair	*Stuhl*
champion	*Meister, Wettkampfsieger, Champion*
challenge	*Herausforderung*
chance	*Gelegenheit*
(to) change	*wechseln, tauschen; Wechsel, Veränderung*
(to) change a tyre	*einen Reifen wechseln*
changing room	*Umkleidekabine*
channel	*Kanal*

(to) charge	*(Geld) verlangen; anklagen*
chart	*Tabelle, Diagramm*
(to) chase	*verfolgen*
(to) chat	*schwätzen; Unterhaltung*
cheap	*billig, günstig*
(to) cheat	*betrügen, schummeln*
(to) check	*kontrollieren*
(to) check in	*sich anmelden*
cheek	*Backe, Wange*
(to) cheer	*anfeuern*
cheese	*Käse*
chemistry	*Chemie*
cheque	*Scheck*
chess	*Schach*
chicken	*Huhn, Hähnchen*
chief	*oberste(r), wichtigste(r), Haupt-*
child	*Kind*
childhood	*Kindheit*
chin	*Kinn*
chips [BE]	*Pommes Frites*
chocolate	*Schokolade*
choice	*(Aus)Wahl*
choir	*Chor*
(to) choose	*wählen, aussuchen*
Christ	*Christus*
Christmas	*Weihnachten*
church	*Kirche*
cinema	*Kino*
circle	*Kreis*
circumstance	*Umstand*
circus	*runder Platz, Zirkus*
citizen	*(Staats)Bürger(in)*
city	*(Groß)Stadt*
(to) claim	*Anspruch erheben auf; behaupten*
(to) clap	*(Beifall) klatschen*
class	*Kategorie*
classmate	*Klassenkamerad(in)*
classroom	*Klassenzimmer*
clause	*Gliedsatz, Nebensatz*
(to) clean	*putzen; sauber*
clear	*klar*
clearly	*klar, deutlich*
clerk	*Angestellte(r), Büroangestellte(r)*
clever	*begabt*
(to) click	*(an)klicken*
cliff	*Klippe*
(to) climb	*klettern*
clock	*Uhr*
(to) close	*schließen, zumachen*
close (to)	*nahe, eng, dicht (bei)*
closed	*geschlossen, zu*
closely	*eng*
cloth	*Tuch, Stoff*
clothes	*Kleider*
cloud	*Wolke*

cloudy	*bewölkt*
club	*Klub*
clue	*Hinweis, Anhaltspunkt*
coach	*Reisebus; Trainer(in)*
coast	*Küste*
coat	*Mantel*
coffee	*Kaffee*
coke	*Coca-Cola*
cold	*kalt, Kälte, Erkältung*
(to) collect	*sammeln, ansammeln*
collection	*Sammlung*
college	*Hochschule, Fachschule*
colour	*Farbe*
column	*Säule, Spalte*
combination	*Verkettung, Verbindung*
(to) combine	*verbinden*
(to) come	*kommen*
comfort	*Behaglichkeit, Trost*
comfortable	*bequem*
(to) comment	*sich zu etw. äußern, einen Kommentar abgeben; Kommentar*
(to) commit	*(ein Verbrechen) begehen, verüben*
(to) have sth. in common	*etwas gemeinsam haben*
common sense	*gesunder Menschenverstand*
(to) communicate	*etwas mitteilen*
communication	*Verständigung*
community	*Gemeinde, Gemeinschaft*
company	*Unternehmen, Firma; Gesellschaft*
(to) compare	*vergleichen*
(to) compete	*konkurrieren*
competition	*Wettbewerb*
(to) complain	*sich beschweren, sich beklagen*
complaint	*Beschwerde, Klage*
(to) complete	*vervollständigen*
completely	*völlig*
complicated	*kompliziert*
comprehensive school	*Gesamtschule*
(to) concentrate	*sich konzentrieren*
concentration	*Konzentration*
(to) concern	*jdn. angehen, betreffen*
concerned	*besorgt, betroffen*
concerning	*bezüglich*
conclusion	*(Schluss)Folgerung*
condition	*Zustand; Bedingung*
(to) conduct	*durchführen, ausführen*
confidence	*Vertrauen*
confident	*zuversichtlich*

(to) confirm	*bestätigen, bekräftigen*
conformation	*Bestätigung*
(to) confuse	*verwirren*
confused	*verwirrt, durcheinander*
confusing	*verwirrend*
(to) congratulate	*beglückwünschen, gratulieren*
Congratulation!	*Gratulation!*
(to) connect	*verbinden*
connected	*verbunden sein*
connection	*Verbindung*
(to) consider	*betrachten, erwägen*
consideration	*Erwägung*
considering	*wenn man etwas bedenkt …*
(to) consist (of)	*bestehen aus*
constantly	*ständig, dauernd*
(to) consult	*um Rat fragen*
construction	*Bauwerk*
(to) consume	*verbrauchen*
contact	*Verbindung*
(to) contain	*enthalten*
content	*Gehalt, Inhalt*
(to) continue	*fortfahren, weitermachen*
contrast	*Gegensatz*
(to) contribute	*etwas zu etwas beisteuern, beitragen*
control	*Kontrolle*
convenient	*bequem, günstig, praktisch*
conversation	*Gespräch*
(to) convince	*jdn. überzeugen*
convinced	*überzeugt*
convincing	*überzeugend*
(to) cook	*kochen, zubereiten; Koch, Köchin*
cooker	*Herd*
cool	*kühl; scharf, stark*
(to) cope	*zurechtkommen*
(to) copy	*abschreiben; kopieren; Kopie, Exemplar*
corner	*Ecke*
(to) correct	*korrigieren, verbessern*
correction	*Korrektur, Verbesserung*
(to) cost	*kosten*
cottage	*kleines Häuschen*
(to) cough	*husten; Husten*
could	*konnte; könnte*
(to) count	*zählen*
country	*Land*
countryside	*Landschaft*
county	*Grafschaft*
couple	*Paar*
a couple of	*zwei; ein paar, einige*
course	*Kurs, Lehrgang*
cousin	*Cousin(e)*

cover	*(Buch)Einband, Deckel*
(to) cover	*bedecken; behandeln, erfassen*
cow	*Kuh*
(to) crash	*zusammenstoßen (mit), hineinfahren (in); Zusammenstoß*
(to) crash into	*prallen gegen*
crazy	*verrückt*
(to) create	*(er)schaffen*
creature	*Lebewesen*
credit card	*Kreditkarte*
crime	*Verbrechen*
crisis	*Krise*
crisps [BE]	*Kartoffelchips*
critic	*Kritiker*
(to) criticise	*kritisch beurteilen*
criticism	*Kritik*
cross	*Kreuz*
crowd	*Menge*
crowded	*überfüllt, voll*
crown	*Krone*
cruel	*grausam*
cruelty	*Grausamkeit*
(to) cry	*weinen; Schrei*
culture	*Kultur*
cup	*Tasse*
cupboard	*Schrank*
curious	*neugierig*
curriculum vitae (CV)	*Lebenslauf*
custom	*Sitte, Brauch*
customer	*Kunde, Kundin*
(to) cut	*schneiden, ausschneiden*
cute	*niedlich, süß*
(to) cycle	*Rad fahren*
CV (curriculum vitae)	*Lebenslauf*
dad	*Papa, Vater*
damage	*Schaden*
damp	*feucht*
(to) dance	*tanzen*
danger	*Gefahr*
dangerous	*gefährlich, gefahrvoll*
(to) dare	*jdn. herausfordern, wagen*
dark	*dunkel, finster*
date	*Verabredung*
daughter	*Tochter*
(to) dawn	*dämmern, tagen; Dämmerung*
day	*Tag*
dead	*tot*
deaf	*taub*
(to) deal	*austeilen, handeln; Abmachung*
dear	*lieb, teuer*
death	*Tod*
debt	*Schulden*

(to) decide	*(sich) entschließen, entscheiden*
decision	*Entscheidung*
declaration	*Erklärung*
(to) declare	*(öffentlich) erklären*
deep	*tief*
defeat	*Niederlage*
defence	*Verteidigung*
(to) defend	*verteidigen*
definite	*sicher, bestimmt*
definitely	*bestimmt, sicherlich*
degree	*Grad*
deliberate	*wohlüberlegt; vorsätzlich*
delicate	*zart, zerbrechlich*
delight	*Vergnügen*
(to) deliver	*liefern; (eine Rede) halten*
demand	*Nachfrage*
(to) demonstrate	*etwas zeigen; demonstrieren*
(to) deny	*abstreiten, bestreiten, leugnen*
(to) depart	*abreisen, abfliegen*
department store	*Kaufhaus*
departure	*Abreise, Abflug*
(to) depend (on, upon)	*abhängen, abhängig sein (von)*
(to) describe	*beschreiben*
description	*Beschreibung*
desert	*Wüste*
(to) deserve	*verdienen*
(to) design	*entwerfen; Entwurf*
desire	*Wunsch*
desk	*Schreibtisch*
desperate	*verzweifelt*
(to) destroy	*zerstören*
detail	*Detail, Einzelheit*
determined	*entschlossen*
(to) develop	*(sich) entwickeln*
development	*Entwicklung*
dialogue	*Dialog*
diary	*Tagebuch, Terminkalender*
dictionary	*Wörterbuch*
(to) die	*sterben*
diet	*Kost, Nahrung*
(to) differ	*sich unterscheiden*
difference	*Unterschied*
different	*verschieden*
difficult	*schwierig*
dining-room	*Esszimmer*
dinner	*Abendessen, Abendbrot*
(to) direct	*leiten, regeln*
direction	*Richtung*
directory	*Inhaltsverzeichnis, Telefonverzeichnis*
dirt	*Schmutz*
dirty	*schmutzig*

disadvantage	*Nachteil*
(to) disagree	*nicht zustimmen*
(to) disappear	*verschwinden*
(to) disappoint	*enttäuschen*
(to) disapprove	*dagegen sein*
(to) discover	*herausfinden, entdecken*
(to) discuss	*besprechen*
disgusting	*empörend, ekelhaft*
dish	*Schale, Schüssel; Platte; Gericht*
dishes [Pl.]	*Geschirr*
(to) dislike	*nicht mögen; Abneigung*
display	*(Schaufenster)Auslage*
distance	*Entfernung*
distant	*fern*
(to) disturb	*stören*
(to) dive	*tauchen*
diving	*das Tauchen*
(to) divide	*teilen*
division	*Verteilung*
divorced	*geschieden*
doctor	*Arzt, Ärztin*
dog	*Hund*
(to) be on the dole	*Arbeitslosengeld beziehen*
door	*Tür*
(to) double	*verdoppeln*
(to) doubt	*zweifeln; Zweifel*
downstairs	*treppab, die Treppe hinunter, unten*
downtown	*Innenstadt*
(to) draw	*zeichnen; ziehen*
drawing	*Zeichnen, Zeichnung*
(to) dream	*träumen; Traum*
(to) dress	*sich kleiden; Kleid*
(to) drink	*trinken; Getränk*
(to) drive	*fahren; Auffahrt*
driving licence	*Führerschein*
driving test	*Führerscheinprüfung*
(to) drop	*fallen (lassen); Fall, Sturz; Tropfen*
(to) drown	*ertrinken; ertränken*
drug	*Droge, Rauschgift*
(to) dry	*trocknen; trocken*
dull	*langweilig, eintönig*
during	*während*
duty	*Dienst, Pflicht*
each	*jeder, jede, jedes (einzelne)*
ear	*Ohr*
early	*früh*
(to) earn	*(Geld) verdienen*
(to) earn a living	*seinen Lebensunterhalt verdienen*
earth	*Erde*
east	*östlich, Osten*
easy	*leicht, einfach*

(to) eat	*essen*
edge	*Kante, Rand*
education	*Erziehung, Ausbildung*
effect	*Wirkung*
effort	*Anstrengung*
e. g.	*z. B. (zum Beispiel)*
egg	*Ei*
either … or …	*entweder … oder …*
elbow	*Ellbogen*
election	*Wahl*
electric(al)	*elektrisch*
electrician	*Elektriker(in)*
electricity	*Elektrizität*
elephant	*Elefant*
elevator	*Aufzug, Fahrstuhl*
else	*alle anderen, sonst*
e-mail	*E-Mail (elektronischer Brief)*
(to) embarrass	*in Verlegenheit (in eine peinliche Lage) bringen*
embarrassed	*verlegen, peinlich berührt*
embarrassing	*peinlich*
emergency	*Notfall*
emigrant	*Auswanderer(in)*
(to) emigrate	*auswandern*
emigration	*Auswanderung*
emotion	*Gefühl*
emphasis	*Betonung*
(to) emphasize	*betonen*
(to) employ	*beschäftigen, anstellen; verwenden*
empty	*leer*
(to) encourage	*ermutigen*
encyclopaedia	*Lexikon*
end	*Ende*
enemy	*Feind*
energy	*Energie*
engaged	*verlobt*
engine	*Motor, Maschine*
engineer	*Ingenieur(in), Techniker(in)*
(to) enjoy	*genießen*
enjoyable	*angenehm, nett, unterhaltsam*
enough	*genügend, ausreichend*
(to) enter	*betreten; einreisen in; teilnehmen an*
enough	*genug*
entertainment	*Unterhaltung*
enthusiastic	*begeistert*
entrance	*Eingang*
entry	*Eintritt*
environment	*Umwelt*
equal	*gleich*
equality	*Gleichheit*
equipment	*Ausrüstung*

eraser [AE]	*Radiergummi*
error	*Fehler*
(to) escape	*entfliehen; Flucht, Ausbruch*
especially	*besonders, insbesondere*
(to) estimate	*(ab)schätzen*
ethnic	*Volks-, ethnisch*
euro	*Euro*
Europe	*Europa*
European	*europäisch; Europäer(in)*
even	*sogar, selbst*
even (number)	*gerade (Zahl)*
evening	*Abend*
event	*Ereignis*
ever	*je, jemals, schon*
every	*jede(r, s)*
everybody	*jede(r)*
everything	*alles*
everywhere	*überall*
exact	*genau*
(to) exaggerate	*übertreiben*
exam(ination)	*Prüfung*
(to) examine	*untersuchen*
example	*Beispiel*
excellent	*ausgezeichnet*
except for	*außer, mit Ausnahme von*
exception	*Ausnahme*
excerpt	*Auszug, Ausschnitt*
(to) exchange	*tauschen; Austausch*
(to) excite	*auf-, erregen*
excited	*aufgeregt*
exciting	*aufregend*
(to) excuse	*entschuldigen*
(to) exercise	*trainieren, üben*
exhibition	*Ausstellung*
(to) exist	*existieren, bestehen*
existence	*Dasein, Leben*
exit	*Ausgang*
(to) expect	*erwarten*
expectation	*Erwartung*
expensive	*teuer*
experience	*Erfahrung*
experienced	*erfahren*
experiment	*Versuch*
(to) explain	*erklären*
explanation	*Erklärung*
(to) explode	*explodieren*
exploration	*Erforschung*
(to) explore	*erforschen*
explosion	*Explosion*
(to) express	*ausdrücken*
expression	*Ausdruck*
extra	*zusätzlich*
extraordinary	*außerordentlich, außergewöhnlich*
extremely	*äußerst, außerordentlich*

eye	*Auge*
(to) face	*sich gegenübersehen; konfrontiert sein mit; Gesicht*
fact	*Tatsache*
factory	*Fabrik*
(to) fail	*(bei einer Prüfung) durchfallen*
failure	*Misserfolg*
fair	*gerecht, fair*
fairly	*ziemlich*
faithful	*treu*
Yours faithfully	*Mit freundlichen Grüßen*
(to) fall	*fallen, stürzen; Absturz*
false	*falsch*
fame	*Ruhm*
familiar	*vertraut*
family	*Familie*
famous	*berühmt*
fantastic	*toll, fantastisch*
far	*von weit her, weit entfernt*
farm	*Bauernhof, Farm*
farther	*weiter (entfernt)*
farthest	*am weitesten (entfernt)*
fashion	*Mode*
fast	*schnell*
(to) fasten	*festmachen*
fat	*fett, dick*
father	*Vater*
fault	*Fehler*
favour	*Gefälligkeit, Gefallen*
favourable	*günstig*
favourite	*Lieblings-*
fax machine	*Faxgerät*
fear	*Angst*
feature	*Merkmal, Eigenschaft; Reportage*
February	*Februar*
(to) be fed up with sth.	*etwas satt haben*
(to) feed	*ernähren, füttern*
(to) feel	*fühlen*
feeling	*Gefühl*
(to) feel sick	*übel sein*
feet	*Füße*
felt-tip pen	*Filzstift*
female	*weiblich*
fence	*Zaun*
ferry	*Fähre*
(to) fetch	*holen*
fever	*Fieber*
few	*wenig(e)*
field	*Wiese, Feld*
fierce	*heftig, scharf, grimmig*
fight	*Kampf*
figure	*Gestalt; Zahl*

file	*Reihe; Aktenordner*
(to) fill	*füllen*
final	*letzte(r, s), endgültig*
finally	*schließlich*
find	*finden*
fine	*Geldstrafe*
fine	*gut, fein, schön*
finger	*Finger*
(to) finish	*enden, aufhören*
(to) fire	*entlassen, feuern; Feuer*
fireman	*Feuerwehrmann*
firm	*Firma*
first	*erste(r,s)*
fish	*Fisch*
fish fingers	*Fischstäbchen*
(to) fit	*(Kleidung) passen*
fix	*fest*
(to) fix	*befestigen, reparieren, in Ordnung bringen*
flag	*Fahne, Flagge*
flame	*Flamme*
(to) flash	*aufleuchten, blinken; (Foto)Blitz*
flat	*flach*
flat	*Wohnung*
(to) flatter	*schmeicheln*
flavour	*Geschmack*
(to) flee	*fliehen*
flight	*Flug, Flucht*
(to) float	*(an der Oberfläche) schwimmen*
(to) flood	*überfluten; Flut, Hochwasser*
floor	*Fußboden; Stockwerk*
flour	*Mehl*
(to) flow	*fließen*
flower	*Blume*
(to) fly	*fliegen*
(to) fold	*falten*
(to) follow	*folgen*
fond	*liebevoll*
food	*Essen, Nahrung*
fool	*Narr, Dummkopf*
foot	*Fuß*
football	*Fußball*
for good	*endgültig*
(to) force	*zwingen; Gewalt*
foreign	*ausländisch*
forest	*Wald*
forever	*für immer*
(to) forget	*vergessen*
(to) forgive	*jdm. verzeihen*
fork	*Gabel*
(to) form	*bilden; Form; Formular*
formal	*förmlich, formell*
former	*früher, ehemalig*
fortunate	*glücklich*
fortune	*Vermögen*

forward	*nach vorn*
(to) found	*gründen*
frame	*Rahmen*
(to) frame	*reinlegen; rahmen; Rahmen*
freak	*Fanatiker(in)*
free	*frei*
free of charge	*kostenlos, gratis*
freedom	*Freiheit*
(to) freeze	*(er)frieren, gefrieren, erstarren*
freight	*Güter, Fracht*
French fries [AE]	*Pommes frites*
frequent	*häufig*
frequently	*oft, häufig*
fresh	*frisch*
friend	*Freund(in)*
friendly	*freundlich*
(to) frighten	*jdn. erschrecken, jdm. Angst machen*
frightened	*verängstigt*
from	*aus, von*
front	*Vorderseite*
frontier	*Grenzland, Grenze*
(to) frown	*die Stirn runzeln*
fruit	*Obst, Früchte, Frucht*
frustrated	*enttäuscht; frustriert*
full	*voll*
fun	*Spaß*
funny	*lustig, witzig*
furniture	*Möbel*
further	*weiter (entfernt), ferner*
furthest	*am weitesten (entfernt)*
future	*Zukunft*
gadget	*Gerät, Apparat*
game	*Spiel*
gang	*Bande, Truppe*
garage	*Garage; Werkstatt*
gap	*Lücke*
garbage	*Müll*
gas [AE]	*Benzin*
gate	*Tor, Sperre; Flugsteig*
(to) gather	*sammeln*
general	*allgemein*
generally	*im Allgemeinen*
generation	*Generation, Menschenalter*
generous	*großzügig*
gentle	*sanft, leicht*
genuine	*echt*
geography	*Geographie, Erdkunde*
(to) get off	*aussteigen*
(to) get ready	*sich fertig machen*
(to) get rid of	*los werden*
(to) get up	*aufstehen*
(to) get used to	*sich gewöhnen an*
ghost	*Geist, Gespenst*

gigantic	*riesig, gigantisch*
giant	*Riese*
gift	*Gabe, Begabung*
girl	*Mädchen*
girlfriend	*Freundin*
(to) give	*geben*
(to) give a hand	*behilflich sein*
(to) give up	*aufgeben, aufhören*
glad	*froh, erfreut, freudig*
glass	*Glas*
glasses	*Brille*
glue	*Klebstoff*
(to) go	*gehen, fahren*
(to) go for a ride	*eine Spazierfahrt machen*
(to) go on holiday	*in Urlaub fahren*
goal	*Ziel, Tor*
gold	*Gold*
goldfish	*Goldfisch*
good-bye	*Auf Wiedersehen, Lebe wohl!*
goods	*Waren, Güter*
(to) govern	*regieren*
government	*Regierung*
grade	*Rang, Note; Jahrgangsstufe*
gradually	*allmählich*
grammar school	*Gymnasium*
grand	*prächtig, großartig*
(to) grant	*gewähren, bewilligen*
grape	*(Wein)Traube*
grass	*Gras*
gravy	*(Braten)Soße*
grateful	*dankbar*
great	*groß, großartig*
green	*grün*
greeting	*Begrüßung, Gruß*
grey [AE], gray [BE]	*grau*
(to) groan	*stöhnen, ächzen*
ground	*(Erd)Boden*
group	*Gruppe*
(to) grow	*wachsen*
growth	*Wachstum*
(to) guard	*bewachen; Wache*
(to) guess	*(er)raten, vermuten; Vermutung*
guest	*Gast*
guitar	*Gitarre*
(to) guide	*führen, leiten; Führer(in), Reiseleiter(in)*
guilty	*schuldig*
gun	*(Schuss)Waffe*
guy	*Typ, Bursche*
habit	*Gewohnheit, Angewohnheit*
(to) hack	*hacken, zerstückeln; in Computer eindringen*
hair	*Haar*

hairdresser	*Friseur(in)*
half	*halb; Hälfte*
hall	*Diele*
ham	*Schinken*
hand	*Hand*
(to) handle	*handhaben, behandeln*
(to) hang	*aufhängen*
(to) happen	*sich ereignen*
happy	*glücklich, froh*
harbour	*Hafen*
hard	*hart, schwer*
hardly	*kaum*
hardware	*Eisenwaren; Computerhardware*
(to) harm	*schaden; Schaden*
harvest	*Ernte*
hat	*Hut*
(to) hate	*hassen; Hass*
(to) have	*haben*
(to) have a shower	*sich duschen*
(to) have a party	*feiern*
(to) have sth. in common	*etwas gemeinsam haben*
head	*Kopf*
headline	*Schlagzeile, Überschrift*
headmaster	*Schulleiter(in), Direktor(in)*
headteacher	*Schulleiter(in)*
headword	*Stichwort (in einem Lexikon), Eintrag*
health	*Gesundheit*
healthy	*gesund*
(to) hear	*hören*
heart	*Herz*
heat	*Hitze*
heavy	*schwer*
height	*Höhe, Größe*
Hello!	*Hallo; Guten Tag!*
helmet	*Helm*
(to) help	*helfen; Hilfe*
Help yourself!	*Greif zu! Bedien dich!*
cannot help doing sth.	*nicht anders können, einfach müssen*
her	*sie, ihr*
here	*hier*
hero	*Held*
heroine	*Heldin*
hers	*ihre(r, s)*
herself	*sich*
(to) hesitate	*zögern, zaudern*
(to) hide	*verbergen*
high	*hoch*
hill	*Hügel*
him	*ihn*
(to) hire	*mieten*
his	*sein(e, s)*
history	*Geschichte*
(to) hit	*schlagen*

(to) hold	*halten; Halt*
hole	*Loch*
holiday	*Urlaub*
holiday job	*Ferienjob*
holy	*heilig*
hollow	*hohl*
home	*Zuhause*
honest	*ehrlich*
honey	*Honig*
honeymoon	*Flitterwochen*
honour	*Ehre*
(to) hope	*hoffen; Hoffnung*
horrible	*grauenhaft, scheußlich*
horse	*Pferd*
hospital	*Krankenhaus*
hostel	*Heim, Herberge*
hostage	*Geisel*
hot	*heiß*
hotel	*Hotel*
hour	*Stunde*
house	*Haus*
household	*Haushalt*
however	*jedoch*
(to) hug	*umarmen; Umarmung*
huge	*riesig*
human	*menschlich*
hunger	*Hunger*
hungry	*hungrig*

(to) hunt	*jagen*
(to) hurry	*sich beeilen; Eile*
(to) hurt	*verletzen*
husband	*Ehemann*
ice	*Eis*
ice-cream	*Speiseeis*
idea	*Vorstellung*
ideal	*vorbildlich*
identity	*Identität*
if	*wenn, falls*
(to) ignore	*nicht beachten*
ill	*krank*
illegal	*ungesetzlich, rechtswidrig*
illness	*Krankheit*
image	*Ebenbild, Bild*
imagination	*Fantasie*
(to) imagine	*sich vorstellen*
immediate	*unmittelbar, sofort*
immense	*ungeheuer, unermesslich*
immigrant	*Einwanderer(in)*
(to) immigrate	*einwandern*
immigration	*Einwanderung*
impatient	*ungeduldig*
importance	*Wichtigkeit*
important	*wichtig*
impossible	*unmöglich*
(to) impress	*imponieren, beeindrucken*

impression	*Eindruck*
impressive	*beeindruckend*
(to) improve	*(sich) verbessern, vorankommen*
improvement	*Verbesserung*
in favour of	*für*
in general	*im Allgemeinen*
(to) include	*einschließen, enthalten, umfassen*
(to) increase	*zunehmen, steigen*
increase	*Erhöhung, Zunahme*
increasing	*zunehmend, steigend*
indeed	*in der Tat, gewiss*
independence	*Unabhängigkeit*
independent	*unabhängig*
Independence Day	*(US) Unabhängigkeitstag (4. Juli)*
Indian	*indisch, Inder; indianisch, Indianer*
indoor	*drinnen, im Haus*
industry	*Industrie*
industrial	*industriell*
influence	*Einfluss*
(to) inform	*benachrichtigen*
informal	*locker*
information	*Information*
injection	*Injektion, Spritze*
(to) injure	*verletzen*
injury	*Verletzung*
(to) inquire (enquire)	*sich erkundigen*
inside	*drinnen*
(to) insist	*bestehen*
instead of	*statt dessen, anstatt*
instruction	*Anweisung, Gebrauchsanweisung*
instrument	*Instrument*
insurance	*Versicherung*
intelligent	*klug, intelligent*
(to) intend	*beabsichtigen*
interest	*Interesse; Zins*
interested in	*interessiert an*
(to) interrupt	*unterbrechen*
interview	*Interview; Vorstellungsgespräch*
(to) introduce	*(jdn., sich) vorstellen*
invitation	*Einladung*
(to) invite	*einladen*
(to) involve	*verwickeln*
irregular	*unregelmäßig*
island	*Insel*
issue	*Streitfrage*
item	*Ding, Stück*
its	*sein, seine*
jacket	*Jacke, Sacco*
jam	*Marmelade*
January	*Januar*
jar	*Glas, Topf*
jealous (of)	*eifersüchtig (auf)*

Jew	*Jude, Jüdin*
jewellery	*Schmuck*
job	*Stellung, Arbeitsstelle*
(to) join	*sich anschließen, beitreten, mitmachen*
joke	*Witz*
journalist	*Journalist(in)*
journey	*Reise*
judge	*Richter(in)*
juice	*Saft*
July	*Juli*
(to) jump	*springen; Sprung*
June	*Juni*
junk food	*Nahrung ohne Nährwert*
just	*nur, bloß; einfach*
justice	*Gerechtigkeit*
(to) justify	*rechtfertigen*
keen on	*scharf auf*
(to) keep	*(be)halten*
(to) keep s.o. waiting	*jdn. warten lassen*
key	*Schlüssel*
keyboard	*Tastatur*
keyword	*Schlüsselwort*
(to) kick	*treten; Tritt*
kid	*Kind*
(to) kill	*töten*
kind	*Art*
kind	*freundlich, liebenswürdig*
kindness	*Freundlichkeit, Liebenswürdigkeit*
king	*König*
kingdom	*Königreich*
kiss	*Kuss*
kitchen	*Küche*
kite	*Drachen*
knife	*Messer*
(to) knock	*klopfen*
(to) know	*wissen*
knowledge	*Kenntnisse, Wissen*
label	*Etikett*
(to) labour	*arbeiten, schuften; Arbeit*
labourer	*Arbeiter, Arbeitskraft*
ladder	*Leiter*
lady	*Dame*
lake	*(Binnen)See*
lamp	*Lampe*
land	*Land*
language	*Sprache*
large	*groß, umfangreich*
(to) last	*dauern*
late	*spät*
lately	*kürzlich, in letzter Zeit*
latest	*neuesten*
(to) laugh	*lachen*

laughter	*Gelächter*
laundry	*Wäscherei*
law	*Gesetz*
(to) lay	*legen; (den Tisch) decken*
lazy	*faul, träge*
(to) lead	*führen*
leaf	*Blatt*
leaflet	*Prospekt, Flugblatt*
(to) learn	*lernen*
least	*am wenigsten*
(to) leave	*verlassen*
(to) be left	*übrig sein*
left	*links*
leg	*Bein*
legal	*gesetzlich zulässig, legal*
legend	*Legende*
lemon	*Zitrone*
lemonade	*Limonade*
(to) lend	*etw. verleihen*
length	*Länge*
less	*weniger*
lesson	*Unterrichtsstunde*
(to) let	*lassen, erlauben; vermieten*
lethal	*tödlich*
letter	*Brief*
letter of application	*Bewerbungsschreiben*
letter to the editor	*Leserbrief*
lettuce	*(Kopf)Salat*
level	*Höhe, Niveau*
liberty	*Freiheit*
library	*Bücherei*
licence	*Genehmigung*
(to) lie	*lügen; liegen*
life, lives [Pl.]	*Leben*
(to) lift	*heben; Aufzug, Lift*
light	*leicht*
(to) light	*anzünden; Licht*
like	*als ob, wie*
(to) like	*mögen*
likely	*wahrscheinlich*
(to) limit	*begrenzen; Begrenzung, Limit*
line	*Zeile, Reihe, Leitung*
(to) link	*verbinden; Verbindung*
lion	*Löwe*
liquid	*Flüssigkeit*
(to) list	*auflisten; Liste*
(to) listen	*hören (Radio)*
litre	*Liter*
little	*klein*
(to) live	*leben*
live	*direkt (TV- oder Radiosendung)*
(to) live together	*zusammen wohnen*

iving room	*Wohnzimmer*
to) load	*ein-, auf-, beladen; Ladung*
ocal	*örtlich*
to) lock	*zuschließen; (Tür-) Schloss*
ocker	*Schließfach*
to) log in	*sich bei einem Computer anmelden*
onely	*einsam, allein*
ong	*lang*
to) long (for)	*sich sehen (nach)*
to) look	*schauen, sehen*
to) look after	*sich kümmern*
to) look for	*suchen*
to) look forward to	*sich freuen auf*
ose	*locker, lose*
rry	*Lastwagen*
to) lose	*verlieren*
ss	*Verlust*
t	*viel*
ud	*laut*
o) love	*lieben; Liebe*
vely	*schön, herrlich, hübsch*
w	*niedrig; leise (Stimme)*
ck	*Glück*
ood luck!	*Viel Glück!*
o) be lucky	*Glück haben*

lunch	*Mittagessen*
lunch time	*Mittagspause*
machine	*Maschine*
mad	*verrückt*
magazine	*Zeitschrift*
mail	*Post*
mailbox	*Briefkasten*
main	*Haupt-*
mainly	*hauptsächlich*
major	*größer, wichtiger*
majority	*Mehrheit*
(to) make	*machen*
(to) make a speech	*eine Rede halten*
male	*männlich*
man	*Mann; Mensch*
(to) manage	*(etwas) fertig bringen; leiten*
manager	*Leiter(in), Direktor(in)*
manual	*Handbuch, Hand-*
many	*viel*
map	*Landkarte, Stadtplan*
March	*März*
(to) march	*marschieren*
mark	*(Schul)Note*
market	*Markt*
marmalade	*(Orangen)Marmelade*
marriage	*Heirat, Ehe*

married	*verheiratet*
(to) marry	*heiraten*
mask	*Maske*
mass	*(kirchliche) Messe*
(to) match	*(farblich) passen*
match	*Spiel, Wettkampf; Streichholz*
mate	*Kamerad(in), Kumpel*
material	*Material*
maths	*Mathe*
matter	*Angelegenheit*
(to) matter	*von Bedeutung sein; Angelegenheit*
May	*Mai*
may	*dürfen*
maybe	*vielleicht*
maze	*Irrgarten*
me	*mir, mich*
meal	*Mahlzeit*
(to) mean	*bedeuten*
meaning	*Sinn, Bedeutung*
means	*Mittel*
means of communication	*Kommunikationsmittel*
meanwhile	*inzwischen, unterdessen*
(to) measure	*messen; Maßnahme*
meat	*Fleisch*
mechanic	*Mechaniker(in)*
media	*die Medien*
(to) meet	*(sich) treffen*
meeting	*Treffen, Versammlung, Zusammenkunft*
(to) melt	*schmelzen*
member	*Mitglied*
memory	*Gedächtnis*
(to) mend	*reparieren, ausbessern*
(to) mention	*erwähnen*
menu	*Speisekarte*
(to) mess	*durcheinander bringen; Unordnung*
message	*Nachricht, Botschaft*
messenger	*Laufbursche, Bote, Bürobote*
metal	*Metall*
microphone	*Mikrofon*
microwave	*Mikrowelle*
midday	*Mittags-, Mittagsze…*
middle	*Mitte*
midnight	*Mitternacht*
might	*könnte*
mile	*Meile*
milk	*Milch*
mind	*Sinn, Verstand*
(to) mind	*ausmachen (in Sätze… wie: Es macht mir nichts aus …)*
mine	*meine(r, s)*
mine	*Bergwerk*

miner	*Bergarbeiter(in)*
mineral water	*Mineralwasser*
minimum wage	*Mindestlohn*
minority	*Minderheit*
minute	*Minute; winzig*
miserable	*elend, unglücklich, erbärmlich*
misfit	*Außenseiter(in)*
(to) miss	*verpassen, vermissen*
mission	*Einsatz, Mission*
mist	*Dunst, Nebel*
mistake	*Fehler, Irrtum*
(to) mix	*mischen*
mixture	*Mischung*
(to) moan	*stöhnen, jammern*
mobile home	*Wohnmobil*
mobile phone	*Handy*
model	*Modell*
moderate	*gemäßigt, mäßig*
moment	*Augenblick*
Monday	*Montag*
money	*Geld*
monkey	*Affe*
monster	*Ungeheuer*
month	*Monat*
mood	*Laune*
moon	*Mond*
moose	*Elch*
more	*mehr, weitere*

morning	*Morgen*
most	*die meisten*
mother	*Mutter*
motion	*Bewegung*
motorbike	*Motorrad*
motorcyclist	*Motorradfahrer(in)*
mountain	*Berg*
mouse	*Maus*
mouth	*Mund*
(to) move	*sich bewegen, umziehen; Bewegung, Zug*
movie	*Film*
movement	*Bewegung*
much	*viel*
mud	*Schlamm*
mug	*Becher*
mum	*Mutti, Mama*
(to) murder	*ermorden; Mord*
murderer	*Mörder(in)*
muscle	*Muskel*
music	*Musik*
musician	*Musiker(in)*
mustn't	*darf nicht*
my	*mein(e,s)*
mysterious	*geheimnisvoll*
mystery	*Geheimnis, Rätsel*
(to) name	*nennen, benennen; Name*
narrow	*eng, schmal*

native	*einheimisch, (Ur)Einwohner(in)*
naturally	*natürlich*
nature	Natur
near	*nahe, in der Nähe*
nearly	*fast, beinahe*
neat	*ordentlich, sauber*
necessary	*nötig, notwendig*
(to) need	*brauchen;* Bedürfnis, Bedarf;
needn't	*braucht nicht, muss nicht*
negative	*negativ, ablehnend*
neighbourhood	Nachbarschaft
neither	*keine (r, s)*
nephew	Neffe
nerve	Nerv
nervous	*nervös, aufgeregt, ängstlich*
net	Netz
never	*nie*
new	*neu*
news	Nachrichten(sendung)
newspaper	Tageszeitung
next	*nächste(r, s)*
next to	*neben*
nice	*schön, angenehm*
nickname	Spitzname
niece	Nichte
night	Nacht
nightmare	Alptraum
nil	Null
noble	*edel, großzügig*
nobody	*niemand*
noise	Lärm, Krach
noisy	*laut, lärmend*
(to) nominate	*nominieren, aufstellen*
none	*keine(r, s)*
nonsense	Unsinn
nor	*auch nicht*
nor do I	*ich auch nicht*
nose	Nase
not yet	*noch nicht*
(to) note	*beachten;* Notiz
note	Notiz
notebook	Notizbuch; *tragbarer* Computer
nothing	*nichts*
(to) notice	*jdn./etwas bemerken*
notice board	Anschlagtafel, *schwarzes* Brett
nought	*null*
now	*jetzt*
nowadays	*heutzutage*
nowhere	*nirgends, nirgendwo*
number	Zahl
nurse	Krankenschwester, Krankenpfleger(in)
nut	Nuss

object	*Objekt, Gegenstand, Ziel*
(to) object	*Einspruch erheben*
(to) observe	*beobachten*
(to) obtain	*erhalten*
obvious	*deutlich, offensichtlich*
occasion	*Anlass*
(to) occur	*geschehen*
October	*Oktober*
of course	*natürlich, selbstverständlich*
offence	*Vergehen*
(to) offend	*beleidigen*
offer	*Angebot; anbieten*
office	*Büro*
office hours	*Bürozeiten*
officer	*Offizier, Beamter*
official	*offiziell, amtlich*
often	*oft, häufig*
oil	*Öl*
old	*alt*
old-fashioned	*altmodisch*
on the dole	*stempeln gehen*
once	*einmal*
ne	*ein(e, s)*
nion	*Zwiebel*
nly	*nur*
pen	*draußen*
(to) operate	*bedienen; operieren*

opinion	*Meinung, Ansicht*
opponent	*Gegner(in)*
opportunity	*(günstige) Gelegenheit*
(to) oppose	*sich wenden gegen, gegen etwas sein*
opposite	*gegenüber, entgegengesetzt; das Gegenteil*
opposition	*Widerstand*
orchestra	*Orchester*
order	*Auftrag*
ordinary	*gewöhnlich*
organisation	*Organisation*
(to) organize	*organisieren*
origin	*Ursprung*
original	*original*
otherwise	*sonst*
ought to	*sollte (eigentlich)*
ours	*unsere(r, s)*
outdoor	*im Freien*
outfit	*Kleider, Kleidung*
outside	*außen, außerhalb*
over	*über*
(to) overcome	*überwinden*
overcrowded	*überfüllt; überbevölkert*
overseas	*Auslands-, ausländisch*
(to) overtake	*überholen*
(to) overwhelm	*überwältigen*
(to) own	*besitzen*

owner	Besitzer(in)
(to) pack	packen einpacken; Bündel
packet	Paket
page	Seite
pain	Schmerz
painful	schmerzhaft
pair	Paar
palace	Palast
pale	bleich, blass
paper	Papier
parade	Parade, Umzug
paragraph	Absatz
paramedic	Sanitäter(in)
pardon	wie bitte?
parent, parents	Elternteil, Eltern
(to) park	(Auto) parken
parliament	Parlament
part	Teil
part-time	Teilzeit
party	Partei; Feier
(to) pass	vorbeigehen (an)
passage	Gang
passenger	Reisende(r), Fahrgast, Passagier
passport	Reisepass, Pass
password	Parole, Passwort
past	vorüber, vorbei
pastime	Zeitvertreib
path	Weg
patience	Geduld
patient	geduldig
pattern	Muster
pause	Pause
pavement	Gehweg, Fußweg
(to) pay	bezahlen, Bezahlung
payment	Zahlung, Bezahlung
pay rise	Gehaltserhöhung
PE (Physical Education)	Sport, Turnen
pea	Erbse
peace	Friede
peaceful	friedlich
peanut	Erdnuss
pen	Feder
pencil	Bleistift
pencil-case	Federmäppchen
people	Menschen, Leute
per cent	Prozent
perfect	vollkommen
(to) perform	aufführen, vorführen
performance	(Film, Theater)Vorstellung; Leistung
perhaps	vielleicht
period	Zeitspanne
persecution	Verfolgung
permission	Erlaubnis
personnel	Personal, Belegschaft
(to) persuade	überzeugen, überreden

pet	*Haustier*
petrol	*Benzin*
(to) phone	*anrufen; Telefon*
phrase	*Wendung, Ausdruck*
physical	*körperlich*
Physical Education (PE)	*Sport, Turnen*
physical science	*Naturwissenschaft*
physics	*Physik*
(to) pick	*(Früchte) pflücken; etwas abholen; aufheben*
picnic	*Picknick*
picture	*Bild*
piece	*Stück*
pig	*Schwein*
(to) pile	*auftürmen; Menge, Haufen*
pilgrim	*Pilger(in)*
pill	*Tablette*
pilot	*Pilot(in)*
pin	*Stecknadel, Anstecker*
pine	*Kiefer*
pink	*rosa*
pipe	*Pfeife*
(to) pity	*bemitleiden; Mitleid*
place	*Platz, Ort, Stelle*
plain	*einfach, schlicht*
(to) plan	*planen; Plan*
plane	*Flugzeug; Fläche, Ebene*
planet	*Planet*
(to) plant	*pflanzen; Pflanze; Fabrikanlage, Werk*
plate	*Teller*
platform	*Bahnsteig*
(to) play	*spielen; Spiel; Theaterstück*
pleasant	*angenehm*
(to) please	*jdm. gefallen*
pleased	*zufrieden*
pleasure	*Vergnügen*
plenty	*zahlreich, mehr als genug*
plug	*Stecker*
pm	*nachmittags, abends*
pocket	*Tasche*
poem	*Gedicht*
(to) point	*zeigen, deuten (auf); Spitze; Punkt, Aussage*
poison	*Gift*
police	*Polizei*
(to) polish	*polieren; Politur*
polite	*höflich*
political	*politisch*
politician	*Politiker(in)*
politics	*Politik*
(to) pollute	*verschmutzen*
pollution	*(Umwelt)Verschmutzung*
poor	*arm*

popular	*beliebt*
population	*Bevölkerung*
pork	*Schweinefleisch*
port	*Hafen(stadt)*
position	*Stellung, Lage*
positive	*sicher, bestimmt*
(to) possess	*besitzen*
possession	*Besitz*
possibility	*Möglichkeit*
possible	*möglich*
(to) post	*auf die Post geben*
pot	*Kanne, Topf*
potato	*Kartoffel*
(to) pour	*gießen*
power	*Kraft, Stärke*
powerful	*mächtig*
practice	*Übung*
(to) practise	*üben*
(to) praise	*loben; Lob*
(to) pray	*beten*
prayer	*Gebet*
precise	*genau, präzise*
(to) prefer	*(etwas) vorziehen*
preparation	*Vorbereitung*
(to) prepare	*vorbereiten*
(to) present	*überreichen, schenken*
present	*gegenwärtig, momentan; Geschenk*
presenter	*Moderator(in)*
president	*Präsident(in)*
(to) press	*bügeln*
pressure	*(nervlicher) Druck*
pretty	*hübsch; ziemlich*
(to) prevent	*verhindern*
previous	*vorhergehend*
price	*(Bezahl)Preis*
pride	*Stolz*
primary school	*Grundschule*
prime minister	*Premierminister(in)*
prince	*Prinz*
princess	*Prinzessin*
(to) print	*drucken*
printout	*Ausdruck*
prison	*Gefängnis*
prize	*Preis (= Gewinn), Auszeichnung*
probable	*wahrscheinlich*
(to) process	*verarbeiten, bearbeiten; Ablauf*
(to) produce	*herstellen; Produkt*
production	*Herstellung*
profit	*Gewinn*
progress	*Fortschritt*
(to) promise	*versprechen; Versprechen*
(to) pronounce	*aussprechen*
proper	*passend, richtig, geeignet*
properly	*anständig, angemessen*

(to) propose	*vorschlagen*
proof	*Beweis*
(to) protect	*(be)schützen*
protection	*Schutz*
(to) protest	*protestieren; Protest*
proud	*stolz*
(to) prove	*beweisen*
(to) provide	*sorgen (für), versorgen*
public	*öffentlich*
public transport	*öffentliche Verkehrsmittel*
(to) pull down	*(ein Haus) abreißen*
(to) punish	*bestrafen*
pupil	*Schüler(in)*
pure	*rein, pur*
(to) push	*schieben, stoßen*
(to) put	*legen, stellen*
quality	*Qualität, Güte*
quantity	*Menge*
quarter	*Viertel*
queen	*Königin*
(to) question	*in Frage stellen; Frage*
questionnaire	*Fragebogen*
quick	*schnell*
quiet	*still, ruhig*
quite	*ganz, ziemlich*
(to) quote	*zitieren; Zitat*
rabbit	*Kaninchen*
race	*Rasse*
rail	*Bahn, Gleis*
railway	*Eisenbahn, Gleise*
rain	*Regen*
(to) raise	*aufziehen, großziehen*
range	*Auswahl*
rank	*Rang*
rare	*selten*
rarely	*selten, nicht oft*
rat	*Ratte*
rather	*lieber; ziemlich*
(to) rattle	*rütteln*
raw	*roh, unbehandelt*
RE (Religious Education)	*Religion(sunterricht)*
(to) reach	*nach jdm./etwas greifen, erreichen*
(to) react	*reagieren*
reaction	*Reaktion*
(to) read	*lesen*
ready	*fertig, bereit*
real	*wirklich, real*
(to) realise	*erkennen, feststellen*
reality	*Realität, Wirklichkeit*
really	*unbedingt*
reason	*Grund, Anlass*
reasonable	*vernünftig; angemessen*
(to) receive	*erhalten, bekommen*
recent	*jüngst, neulich*
recently	*neulich, in letzter Zeit*

receptionist	*Empfangsdame (im Hotel)*
(to) recognise	*erkennen*
(to) recommend	*empfehlen*
(to) record	*aufzeichnen, aufnehmen*
(to) recover	*wiedererlangen; sich erholen*
(to) recycle	*wieder verwerten, aufbereiten*
red	*rot*
(to) reduce	*herabsetzen, verringern*
(to) refer (to)	*sich beziehen (auf)*
(to) refuse	*abschlagen, sich weigern*
(to) regard	*betrachten*
rehearsal	*Probe*
region	*Region, Bezirk, Bereich*
(to) regret	*bedauern; Bedauern*
regular	*regelmäßig*
(to) reject	*etwas ablehnen*
related	*verbunden, verwandt*
relationship	*Beziehung*
relative	*Verwandte(r)*
(to) relax	*sich ausruhen, entspannen*
reliable	*zuverlässig*
(to) remark	*äußern, bemerken; Bemerkung*
(to) remember	*sich erinnern, denken an*
(to) remind (of)	*jmdn. erinnern (an)*
(to) remove	*beseitigen, entfernen*
(to) rent	*mieten, leihen; Miete*
(to) repair	*reparieren*
(to) repeat	*wiederholen*
(to) replace	*ersetzen*
(to) reply	*antworten, Antwort*
report	*Bericht*
(to) represent	*vertreten*
reputation	*Ruf, Ansehen*
(to) rescue	*retten*
(to) reserve	*reservieren, zurückhalten, aufheben*
respect	*Hinsicht*
responsibility	*Verantwortung*
responsible	*verantwortlich*
rest	*Ruhepause, Rest; ausruhen*
result	*Ergebnis; Note*
(to) return	*zurückkehren; zurücksenden, -bringen*
review	*(Buch, Film)Besprechung*
revision exercise	*Wiederholungsübung*
rhyme	*Reim*
rice	*Reis*
rich	*reich*
(to) ride	*reiten; Fahrt*

(to) ride a bike	*Rad fahren*
right	*richtig, direkt; gerade; rechts*
(to) ring	*klingeln*
(to) rise	*(an-, auf-)steigen; aufgehen (Sonne)*
(to) risk	*riskieren; Risiko*
rival	*Rivale, Rivalin, Konkurrent(in)*
river	*Fluss*
road	*Straße*
(to) rob	*be-, ausrauben*
robot	*Roboter*
rocket	*Rakete*
role	*Rolle*
(to) roll	*rollen*
romantic	*romantisch*
roof	*Dach*
room	*Zimmer, Raum*
rope	*Seil, Tau*
rough	*rau, grob*
round	*rund; um … herum; Runde*
route	*Route, Strecke*
(to) rub	*reiben*
rubber	*Radiergummi*
rubbish	*Müll; Blödsinn*
rude	*unhöflich*
(to) ruin	*ruinieren, zerstören; Ruin, Pleite*

rule	*Bestimmung, Vorschrift*
rumour	*Gerücht*
(to) run	*laufen*
(to) run in the family	*in der Familie liegen*
(to) rush	*eilen, hetzen*
sad	*traurig, betrübt*
safe	*sicher*
safety	*Sicherheit*
(to) sail	*segeln, (mit dem Schiff) fahren, reisen*
salad	*Salat*
salary	*Lohn, Gehalt*
sale	*Verkauf*
same	*der-, die-, dasselbe*
sandwich	*belegtes Brot*
(to) satisfy	*zufrieden stellen*
Saturday	*Samstag*
sausage	*Wurst, Würstchen*
(to) save	*retten; aufbewahren; sparen*
(to) saw	*sägen*
(to) say	*sagen*
scared	*verängstigt, erschrocken*
scarf	*Schal, Halstuch*
scary	*gruselig, unheimlich*
scene	*Szene*
schedule	*Programm*
scholarship	*Stipendium*

school	Schule
school lunch	Mittagessen in der Schule
school report	Zeugnis
science	Naturwissenschaft
scientist	(Natur)Wissenschaftler(in)
scissors	Schere
score	Spielstand
scrapbook	Sammelalbum
(to) scream	schreien; Schrei
screen	Bildschirm
script	Drehbuch
sea	das Meer, die See
seal	Robbe, Seehund
(to) search	suchen; Nachforschung, Suche
seasick	seekrank
at the seaside	am Meer
season	Jahreszeit
second	Sekunde; zweite(r,s)
secret	Geheimnis
secretary	Sekrektär(in)
section	Abschnitt, Teil
seed	Saat, Same
(to) seem	scheinen
(to) sell	verkaufen
(to) send	senden, verschicken
sense	Sinn, Verstand
sense of humor	Sinn für Humor

sensible	vernünftig
sensitive	sensibel, empfindlich
sentence	Urteil(sspruch); Satz
(to) separate	trennen, (ab)teilen
separate	getrennt, abgesondert
separated	getrennt
serious	ernst(haft)
(to) serve	dienen, servieren
(to) serve	servieren
service	Bedienung; Dienst
set	(Fernseh)Apparat; Satz (Set)
(to) settle	sich niederlassen; besiedeln
settlement	Siedlung, Niederlassung
several	mehrere, verschiedene
shade	Schatten
shadow	Schatten
(to) shake	schütteln, zittern
shame	Schande; Schamgefühl
shape	Form, Gestalt
(to) share	teilen
sharp	scharf
shawl	Schultertuch
sheep	Schaf
shelf	Regal
shelter	Schutz
(to) shine	glänzen, scheinen

ship	*Schiff*
shirt	*Hemd*
(to) shock	*einen Schock versetzen, schockieren; Schock*
shoe	*Schuh*
shop	*Laden*
shop assistant	*Verkäufer(in)*
shoplifter	*Ladendieb(in)*
(to) shoot	*schießen, erschießen*
shore	*Küste, Ufer*
short	*kurz*
shorts	*kurze Hosen, Shorts*
shot	*Schuss*
should	*sollte*
(to) shout	*rufen, (an)schreien*
shower	*Dusche*
(to) shut	*schließen*
shy	*schüchtern, scheu*
side	*Seite*
sidewalk [AE]	*Gehweg*
sight	*Anblick*
(to) sign	*unterschreiben; Zeichen*
(to) signal	*blinken; Signal, Zeichen*
signature	*Unterschrift*
silence	*Ruhe, Stille*
silly	*dumm*
simple	*einfach, schlicht*
since	*seit*
Yours sincerely	*Mit freundlichen Grüßen*
single	*einzeln; ledig*
(to) sink	*sinken, untergehen*
sister	*Schwester*
(to) sit	*sitzen*
situation	*Lage, Situation*
size	*Größe*
skilful	*geschickt, gewandt*
skill	*Fähigkeit, Fertigkeit*
skin	*Haut*
skirt	*Rock*
sky	*Himmel*
skyline	*Silhouette, Skyline*
slave	*Sklave, Sklavin*
sledge	*Schlitten*
(to) sleep	*schlafen; Schlaf*
sleeping bag	*Schlafsack*
(to) slide	*gleiten, rutschen*
slight	*schwach, klein, unbedeutend*
(to) slip	*ausrutschen und hinfallen*
slogan	*Werbespruch*
slope	*Hang*
slow	*langsam*
small	*klein*
smart	*schlau, clever, intelligent*

(to) smell	riechen; Geruch
(to) smile	lächeln; Lächeln
(to) smoke	rauchen; Rauch
smooth	glatt
snake	Schlange
(to) snow	schneien; Schnee
so far	bisher
(to) soak	einweichen
soap	Seife
sober	nüchtern
society	Gesellschaft
sock	Socke, Strumpf
soft	weich
soft drink	alkoholfreies Getränk
soil	Erdboden
solar	Sonnen-
solar energy	Sonnenenergie
soldier	Soldat(in)
(to) solve	lösen, auflösen
some	einige, irgendein
somebody	jemand
somehow	irgendwie
sometimes	manchmal
son	Sohn
song	Lied
soon	bald
sore	wund
sorry	es tut mir Leid
sort	Sorte
sound	Ton, Geräusch
soup	Suppe
source	Quelle
space	Raum
(to) spare	jdn. verschonen
spark	Funke
(to) speak	sprechen, reden
(to) speak up	lauter sprechen
speaker	Sprecher(in)
special	besondere
speech	Rede
spectator	Zuschauer(in)
(to) make a speech	eine Rede halten
speed	Geschwindigkeit
speed limit	Geschwindigkeitsbegrenzung
(to) spell	buchstabieren
(to) spend	(Zeit) verbringen; (Geld) ausgeben
spicy	würzig, stark gewürzt
(to) spill	verschütten
(to) spin	schleudern, drehen
spirit	Geist
(to) split	etwas teilen, halbieren
(to) spoil	verderben, verschandeln
spoon	Löffel
(to) spot	entdecken; Fleck
(to) spread	ausbreiten, verteilen

spring	Frühling
square	öffentlicher Platz; Viereck
(to) squash	zerdrücken
stadium	Stadion
stage	Bühne
staff	Personal
stain	Fleck
stall	Stand
stamp	Briefmarke
star	Stern; Star
(to) start	anfangen, beginnen; Anfang, Beginn
state	Staat
statement	Aussage, Behauptung
station	Bahnhof
statue	Statue
status	Status, Rang
(to) stay	beiben; Aufenthalt
steady	stetig; fest; standhaft
(to) steal	stehlen
steam	Dampf
step	Schritt, Stufe
stepmother	Stiefmutter
stick	Zweig
(to) stick	kleben
stiff	steif
still	noch
(to) sting	stechen; Stachel; Stich
(to) stir	(sich) rühren, sich regen
stomach	Magen
stone	Stein
(to) stop	aufhören
store	Laden, Geschäft
(to) store	speichern
store room	Lagerraum
storm	Sturm
story	Geschichte
straight	gerade
strange	fremdartig, seltsam
stream	Bach
street	Straße
strength	Kraft, Stärke
(to) stress	belasten; Stress
(to) stretch	sich erstrecken
strict	streng
strike	Streik
string	Schnur, Bindfaden
strong	stark
(to) struggle	kämpfen; Kampf
(to) get stuck	stecken bleiben
(to) study	erforschen; studieren, lernen; Studie
stuff	Zeug, Kram
stupid	dumm, blöd
subject	Thema, Gegenstand; Schulfach
suburb	Vorort

subway	*U-Bahn [AE], Unterführung [BE]*
(to) succeed	*Erfolg haben*
success	*Erfolg*
successful	*erfolgreich*
such	*solche*
suddenly	*plötzlich, auf einmal*
(to) suffer from	*leiden an*
sugar	*Zucker*
(to) suggest	*vorschlagen*
suggestion	*Anregung, Vorschlag*
(to) suit	*passen; Anzug*
sum	*Summe*
summer	*Sommer*
supermarket	*Supermarkt*
(to) supply	*liefern; Angebot, Vorrat*
(to) support	*ernähren; unterstützen; Unterstützung*
(to) suppose	*annehmen, vermuten*
sure	*natürlich, sicherlich*
surface	*Oberfläche*
(to) surf	*surfen; Brandung*
(to) surprise	*überraschen; Überraschung*
survey	*Umfrage, Studie*
(to) survive	*überleben*
(to) suspect	*verdächtigen, ahnen; Verdächtiger*
(to) swallow	*schlucken*
(to) sweep	*fegen, kehren*
(to) sweat	*schwitzen; Schweiß*
sweet	*süß*
(to) swim	*schwimmen*
(to) swing	*schwingen; Schaukel*
(to) switch	*(um)schalten; Schalter*
table	*Tisch*
(to) take	*nehmen*
(to) take a break	*eine Pause machen*
(to) take part in	*teilnehmen an*
tale	*Erzählung*
talent	*Begabung*
(to) talk	*sprechen; Gespräch*
tall	*hoch, groß*
tape	*Tonband*
target	*Ziel(scheibe)*
task	*Aufgabe*
(to) taste	*schmecken; Geschmack*
tax	*Steuer*
tea	*Tee*
(to) teach	*unterrichten*
team	*Mannschaft*
(to) be on a team	*in einer Mannschaft sein*
(to) tear	*zerreißen, zerren*
technical	*technisch*
technology	*Technologie*
teenager	*Jugendliche(r)*

teeth [Pl. von tooth]	*Zähne*
telephone	*Telefon*
television	*Fernsehgerät*
(to) tell	*erzählen*
temperature	*Temperatur*
tense	*Zeitform*
tent	*Zelt*
term	*Bedingung; Trimester*
terrible	*schrecklich*
(to) test	*(ab)prüfen; Prüfung*
than	*als (nach Komparativ)*
(to) thank	*danken*
Thanksgiving	*amerikanisches Erntedankfest*
theatre	*Theater*
their	*ihr(e)*
theme park	*Freizeitpark, Vergnügungspark*
then	*dann, damals*
theory	*Theorie*
there	*da, dort*
there is/are	*es gibt*
these	*diese*
thief	*Dieb*
hin	*dünn*
hing	*Ding*
to) think	*denken*
hird	*dritte(r, s)*
thirst	*Durst*
thirsty	*durstig*
thorough	*gründlich*
those	*die da, jene dort*
though	*obwohl*
thought	*Gedanke*
thousand	*tausend*
threat	*Bedrohung*
(to) threaten	*bedrohen*
thriller	*Reißer, Krimi*
through	*durch*
(to) throw	*werfen*
thumb	*Daumen*
Thursday	*Donnerstag*
(to) tick	*ankreuzen*
ticket	*Karte*
tidy	*ordentlich*
(to) tie	*binden; Krawatte*
tight	*eng; dicht*
till (until)	*bis*
time	*Zeit*
(to) be on time	*rechtzeitig sein, pünktlich sein*
(to) have a good time	*sich amüsieren*
(to) take time	*dauern, Zeit kosten*
timetable	*Fahrplan*
tin [BE]	*Zinn; Dose, Büchse*
tip	*Trinkgeld; Rat, Tipp*
tired	*müde*

title	Überschrift, Titel
today	heute
toe	Zehe
together	zusammen
tomorrow	morgen
tongue	Zunge; Sprache
tonight	heute Abend
tool	Werkzeug, Gerät
tooth	Zahn
top	oberes Ende, Spitze; Top (Shirt)
topic	Thema
total	Gesamtbetrag, Summe
totally	völlig
(to) touch	berühren; Berührung
tough	zäh
tour (of)	Rundreise (durch)
tourist	Tourist(in)
towards	in Richtung auf
tower	Turm
town	Stadt
toy	Spielzeug
track	(Fuß)Spur
track and field	Leichtathletik
tracksuit	Jogginganzug
(to) trade	handeln; Handel; Beruf
tradition	Überlieferung, Tradition
traffic	Verkehr
traffic jam	(Verkehrs)Stau
train	Zug
trainee	Praktikant(in)
training	Ausbildung
tram	Straßenbahn
(to) translate	übersetzen
translation	Übersetzung
transparency	Folie
transport	Verkehrsmittel
trap	Falle
(to) travel	reisen; Reise
travel agency	Reisebüro
(to) treat	behandeln
treatment	Behandlung
tree	Baum
trend	Richtung
(to) trick	jdm. einen Streich spielen; Streich
trip	Ausflug, Reise
trouble	Problem, Schwierigkeit
trousers	Hose
true	wahr
(to) trust	vertrauen
truth	Wahrheit
(to) try	versuchen; Versuch
tube	Londons U-Bahn; Röhre
Tuesday	Dienstag

tune	*Lied, Melodie*
(to) turn	*drehen; Drehung, Kurve*
TV set	*Fernsehgerät*
on TV	*im Fernsehen*
twice	*zweimal*
twins	*Zwillinge*
typical (of)	*typisch (für)*
unable	*unfähig, nicht in der Lage*
umbrella	*Regenschirm*
uncertain	*unsicher*
uncle	*Onkel*
uncomfortable	*unbequem*
under	*unter*
to) underline	*unterstreichen*
underneath	*unter*
to) understand	*verstehen, begreifen*
to) undo	*öffnen; etwas rückgängig machen*
unemployed	*arbeitslos*
unemployment	*Arbeitslosigkeit*
unfair	*ungerecht, unlauter*
nfortunate	*unglücklich*
nfriendly	*unfreundlich*
nhappy	*unglücklich*
nhealthy	*ungesund*
nimportant	*unwichtig*
nit	*Lektion, Einheit*
o) unite	*(sich) vereinigen*
university	*Universität*
unkind	*unfreundlich*
unknown	*unbekannt, nicht bekannt*
unless	*wenn nicht*
(to) unpack	*auspacken*
unpleasant	*unerfreulich*
unpopular	*unbeliebt*
unsafe	*unsicher*
unskilled	*ungelernt*
unskilled worker	*Hilfsarbeiter(in)*
untidy	*unordentlich*
until	*bis*
unusual	*ungewöhnlich*
unwanted	*unerwünscht, störend*
(to) upset	*aufregen, aufwiegeln; aufgebracht, aufgeregt*
upside-down	*verkehrt herum, auf dem Kopf*
upstairs	*nach oben, oben*
urgent	*dringend*
(to) use	*gebrauchen, nutzen*
useful	*nützlich*
useless	*nutzlos*
usual	*gewöhnlich*
vacation [AE]	*Ferien*
valley	*Tal*
(to) value	*wertschätzen; Wert*
van	*Transporter, Lieferwagen*

vandalism	Zerstörungswut
(to) vanish	verschwinden
variety	Auswahl, Mannigfaltigkeit
various	verschieden
vegetable	Gemüse
vegetarian	Vegetarier(in)
vehicle	Fahrzeug
very	sehr
victim	Opfer
victory	Sieg
view	Ansicht, Meinung; Aussicht
village	Dorf
violence	Gewalt, Gewalttätigkeit
violent	gewalttätig; heftig
virtual	so gut wie; nicht wirklich vorhanden, virtuell
vision	Sehvermögen; Vorstellung, Einbildung
(to) visit	besuchen; Besuch
visitor	Besucher(in)
vocabulary	Wortschatz
voice	Stimme
volleyball	Volleyball
volunteer	Freiwillige(r)
(to) vote	abstimmen; wählen; Stimmrecht, Stimme
voyage	Schiffsreise
wage	Lohn
(to) wait	warten
waiter	Kellner, Ober
waitress	Kellnerin
(to) wake up	aufwachen
(to) walk	gehen; Spaziergang
wall	Wand, Mauer
wallet	Brieftasche
wallpaper	Tapete
(to) want	(haben) wollen
war	Krieg
wardrobe	(Kleider)Schrank
warm	warm
(to) wash	waschen
(to) waste	verschwenden, vergeuden; Abfall, Verlust
waste water	Abwasser
(to) watch	sehen, fernsehen
Watch out!	Achtung!
water	Wasser
wave	Welle
wax	Wachs
way	Weg
weak	schwach
wealth	Wohlstand
wealthy	wohlhabend, reich
weapon	Waffe
(to) wear	(Kleid, Uniform) tragen

weather	*Wetter*
weather forecast	*Wettervorhersage, Wetterbericht*
Wednesday	*Mittwoch*
wedding	*Hochzeit*
wedding anniversary	*Hochzeitstag*
week	*Woche*
weekday	*Wochentag, Werktag*
weekend	*Wochenende*
(to) weigh	*wiegen*
weight	*Gewicht*
welcome	*willkommen*
Welsh	*walisisch, aus Wales*
wet	*nass*
wet paint	*frisch gestrichen*
whale	*Walfisch*
wheel	*Rad*
wheelchair	*Rollstuhl*
when	*wann*
where	*wo*
whereas	*wohingegen, während*
wherever	*wohin auch immer*
whether	*ob*
while	*während*
(to) whisper	*flüstern; Geflüster*
(to) whistle	*pfeifen; Pfeife; Pfiff*
white	*weiß*
whole	*ganz*
wholly	*gänzlich*
wide	*breit*
widow	*Witwe*
widower	*Witwer*
wife	*Ehefrau*
window	*Fenster*
wing	*Flügel; Gebäudetrakt*
(to) wipe	*(ab)wischen, (ab)trocknen*
wire	*Draht*
wise	*weise, klug*
(to) wish	*wünschen; Wunsch*
within	*drin, im Innern, innerhalb*
without	*ohne*
witness	*Zeuge, Zeugin*
woman	*Frau*
(to) wonder	*sich fragen; sich wundern über; Wunder*
wonderful	*wunderbar*
wood	*Holz*
word	*Wort*
(to) be out of work	*arbeitslos sein*
world	*Welt*
worried	*beunruhigt, besorgt*
(to) worry about	*sich Sorgen machen über*
worse	*schlechter, schlimmer*
worst	*der/die/das schlechteste*
worth	*wert (sein)*

wound	*Wunde*
(to) write	*schreiben*
wrong	*falsch, unrecht*
(to) yawn	*gähnen*
year	*Jahr*
yellow	*gelb*
yesterday	*gestern*
young	*jung*
youngster	*Jugendliche(r)*
youth	*Jugendliche(r); Jugend*
(to) zap	*hin- und herschalten*
zero	*Null*
zoo	*Tierpark, Zoo*

Ihre Meinung ist uns wichtig!

Ihre Anregungen sind uns immer willkommen. Bitte informieren Sie uns mit diesem Schein über Ihre Verbesserungsvorschläge!

Titel-Nr.	Seite	Vorschlag

Bitte hier abtrennen

Die echten Hilfen zum Lernen ... **STARK**

Bitte hier abtrennen

Zutreffendes bitte ankreuzen! Die Absenderin/der Absender ist:

- ☐ Lehrer/in in den Klassenstufen: ____
- ☐ Fachbetreuer/in
  Fächer: ____
- ☐ Seminarlehrer/in
  Fächer: ____
- ☐ Regierungsfachberater/in
  Fächer: ____
- ☐ Oberstufenbetreuer/in
- ☐ Schulleiter/in
- ☐ Leiter/in Lehrerbibliothek
- ☐ Leiter/in Schülerbibliothek
- ☐ Referendar/in, Termin 2. Staatsexamen: ____
- ☐ Sekretariat
- ☐ Schüler/in, Klasse: ____
- ☐ Elternteil
- ☐ Sonstiges: ____

STARK Verlag
Postfach 1852
85318 Freising

17-VGR

Bitte ausfüllen und im frankierten Umschlag an uns einsenden. Für Fensterkuverts geeignet.

Kennen Sie Ihre Kundennummer? Bitte hier eintragen.

Absender (Bitte in Druckbuchstaben!)

Name/Vorname

Straße/Nr.

PLZ/Ort

Telefon privat

Geburtsjahr

E-Mail

Schule/Schulstempel (Bitte angeben!)

Unterrichtsfächer: (Bei Lehrkräften!)

(Bitte blättern Sie um)

Gymnasium Mathematik

Zentrale Prüfungen

Bayerischer Mathematik-Test (BMT)
8. Kl. – Gymnasium Bayern .... Best.-Nr. 950081
Bayerischer Mathematik-Test (BMT)
10. Kl. – Gymnasium Bayern .. Best.-Nr. 950001
Vergleichsarbeiten Mathematik 6. Klasse
Gymnasium Baden-W. .... Best.-Nr. 850061
Vergleichsarbeiten Mathematik 8. Klasse
Gymnasium Baden-W. .... Best.-Nr. 850081
Zentrale Klassenarbeit Mathematik 10. Kl.
Gymnasium Baden-W. .... Best.-Nr. 80001
LSE 8 Mathematik NRW, Mecklenburg-Vorp.,
Hamburg .... Best.-Nr. 515081
Zentrale Prüfung Mathematik Klasse 10
Gymnasium NRW .... Best.-Nr. 550001
Mittlerer Schulabschluss Mathematik
Berlin .... Best.-Nr. 111500
Zentrale Prüfung Mathematik Jahrgangsstufe 10
Gymnasium Brandenburg .... Best.-Nr. 1250001
Prüfung zum Übergang in die Jahrgangsstufe 11
Mathematik Jahrgangsstufe 10 Gymnasium/
Gesamtschule Mecklenb.-Vorp. Best.-Nr. 1350001
Besondere Leistungsfeststellung Mathematik
10. Klasse Gymnasium Sachsen Best.-Nr. 1450001
Besondere Leistungsfeststellung Mathematik
10. Klasse Gymn. Thüringen .... Best.-Nr. 1650001

Kompakt-Wissen

Kompakt-Wissen Algebra .... Best.-Nr. 90016
Kompakt-Wissen Geometrie .... Best.-Nr. 90026

Realschule Mathematik

Zentrale Prüfungen

Bayerischer Mathematik-Test (BMT)
6. Klasse – Realschule Bayern .. Best.-Nr. 915061
Bayerischer Mathematik-Test (BMT)
8. Klasse – Realschule Bayern .. Best.-Nr. 915081
Vergleichsarbeiten Mathematik 6. Klasse
Realschule Baden-Württemb. .. Best.-Nr. 815061
Vergleichsarbeiten Mathematik 8. Klasse
Realschule Baden-Württemb. .. Best.-Nr. 815081
LSE 8 Mathematik NRW, Mecklenburg-Vorp.,
Hamburg .... Best.-Nr. 515081
Orientierungsarbeit Mathematik Klasse 8
Mittelschule Sachsen .... Best.-Nr. 1415081

Kompakt-Wissen

Kompakt-Wissen Realschule
Mathematik .... Best.-Nr. 914001

Gymnasium Französisch

Zentrale Prüfungen

Zentrale Klassenarbeit Französisch 10. Klasse
Gymnasium Baden-W. .... Best.-Nr. 80501

Kompakt-Wissen

Kompakt-W. Kurzgrammatik .. Best.-Nr. 945011
Kompakt-W. Grundwortschatz .. Best.-Nr. 905001

Gymnasium Latein

Kompakt-Wissen Gymnasium
Kurzgrammatik .... Best.-Nr. 906011

Geschichte

Kompakt-Wissen Realschule
Geschichte .... Best.-Nr. 914801
Kompakt-Wissen Gymnasium
Geschichte Unter-/Mittelstufe .. Best.-Nr. 907601

Bestellungen bitte direkt an:
STARK Verlagsgesellschaft mbH & Co. KG
Postfach 1852 · 85318 Freising
Telefon 0180 3 179000* · Telefax 0180 3 179001*
www.stark-verlag.de · info@stark-verlag.de
*9 Cent pro Min. aus dem deutschen Festnetz

Die echten Hilfen zum Lernen ...

STARK

17-VGR